0 0051 0033965 7

CITADEL
of
FAITH

By Shoghi Effendi:

GOD PASSES BY
THE ADVENT OF DIVINE JUSTICE
THE PROMISED DAY IS COME

Collections of Letters and Messages:

MESSAGES TO THE BAHÁ'Í WORLD
THE WORLD ORDER OF BAHÁ'U'LLÁH
BAHÁ'Í ADMINISTRATION

Translations:

THE DAWN-BREAKERS
THE KITÁB-I-ÍQÁN
EPISTLE TO THE SON OF THE WOLF
GLEANINGS FROM THE WRITINGS OF BAHÁ'U'LLÁH
PRAYERS AND MEDITATIONS BY BAHÁ'U'LLÁH
THE HIDDEN WORDS OF BAHÁ'U'LLÁH

SHOGHI EFFENDI

CITADEL of FAITH
Messages to America
1947~1957

"*the stalwart occupants of the citadel of the Faith of Bahá'u'lláh have with extraordinary steadfastness, enviable fidelity and magnificent courage, not only shielded the interests, preserved the integrity and demonstrated the worthiness, of the Cause they have embraced, but have sallied forth, with dynamic and irrepressible energy, to implant its banner and establish its outposts in countries and continents far beyond the original scene of their operations.*" —SHOGHI EFFENDI

UNITY SCHOOL LIBRARY
UNITY VILLAGE, MISSOURI 64065

BAHÁ'Í

BAHÁ'Í PUBLISHING TRUST
415 Linden Avenue
Wilmette, Illinois 60091

Copyright © 1965 by the National Spiritual Assembly
of the Bahá'ís of the United States of America
All rights reserved
Third Printing 1980
Standard Book Number: 0-87743-011-x

12/97

Printed in the United States of America

BP
375
E3
1965
c.1

Preface

The communications of Shoghi Effendi, Guardian of the Bahá'í Faith, addressed by him directly to the Bahá'ís of North America between 1932 and 1946 were published by the National Spiritual Assembly of the United States in 1947 under the title "Messages to America, 1932-1946."

This compilation covered a period during which the structure of the Administrative Order of Bahá'u'lláh was firmly established under the infallible guidance of the Guardian, and the foundations laid for the preponderating role which the American Bahá'í Community was destined to assume in the intercontinental and global teaching plans launched by Shoghi Effendi in 1946 and 1953.

In the period from 1950 to 1957 the beloved Guardian addressed a series of majestic messages to the entire Bahá'í world, delineating the unprecedented Ten Year World Crusade and reporting the stirring victories achieved in pursuance of its objectives. The response evoked by these communications in the hearts of the believers everywhere brought about an unprecedented expansion of the Faith, culminating in the world-wide celebrations of the Most Great Jubilee in 1963, the fulfillment of the prophetic pronouncements relating to that date, and made possible the establishment of the Universal House of Justice, that supreme and infallible body which now guides the destinies of the world-wide Bahá'í community. The National Spiritual Assembly of the United States published these messages in 1958 in a volume entitled "Messages to the Bahá'í World, 1950-1957."

In the decade from 1947 to 1957 Shoghi Effendi, in a separate series of messages, repeatedly addressed the American Bahá'ís, describing in challenging terms their world mission, reminding them of their spiritual primacy as the trustees and executors of the Divine Plan of 'Abdu'l-Bahá, and reinforcing that primacy with the mysterious power of accomplishment inherent in his words of encouragement and exhortation.

At this time, when the American Bahá'í Community faces an ever-increasing measure of responsibility as it moves forward to attain the goals of the Nine Year Plan, it is particularly befitting that these communications from the Guardian of the Faith be collected and made available in a single source. The present volume includes all of those messages addressed by Shoghi Effendi directly and exclusively to the Bahá'ís of the United States in the critical and historic years of the last decade of his ministry, a period when the flow of his guidance and inspiration reached its zenith.

It is certain that a careful study of these communications will impart to the reader a profound understanding of the unique character of the mission conferred upon the American Bahá'í Community, not only in foreign fields but on its own home front, and will reveal to the individual members of that favored community a new vision of the nature of that spiritual primacy which is their birthright.

PAUL HANEY

Bahá'í World Center
Haifa, Israel
September 1965

Contents

CITADEL
of
FAITH

Believers' Generous Response to Temple Fund

Thrilled by generous response of believers to Temple Fund. Deeply touched. Hail latest striking evidence of the magnificent spirit, unshakable solidarity and unflinching resolve of American Bahá'í Community. Deepest loving gratitude.

[January 20, 1947]

Call to Fuller Participation

Acclaim with grateful heart evidences of steadily accelerating movement of pioneers, multiplication of conferences, consolidation of activities of national committees, progress in preliminaries of internal ornamentation of Temple, and formulation of teaching policy in southern states. Overwhelmed by tributes paid my own humble efforts by stalwart company whose championship of Faith of Bahá'u'lláh during last quarter century provided greatest support and solace, enabling me to sustain the weight of cares and responsibilities of Guardianship.

Impelled to plead afresh to ponder responsibilities incurred in transatlantic field of service. Time is flying. First year of Second Seven Year Plan is drawing to a close. Shadow of war's tragic aftermath is deepening. Initial stage of colossal task undertaken in European continent still in balance. Urge stress for entire community extreme urgency to reinforce promptly, at whatever cost, however inadequate the instruments, the number of volunteers, both settlers and itinerant teachers, whom posterity will rightly recognize as vanguard of torch-bearers of Bahá'u'lláh's resistless, world-redeeming order to despairing millions of diversified races, conflicting nationalities in darkest, most severely tested, spiritually depleted continent of globe. Prayerfully awaiting response by all ranks of community to supreme call to fuller participation in glorious enterprise.

[January 30, 1947]

Consolidation in Europe

Overjoyed, grateful, proud of notable expansion of manifold activities in three continents. Vital significance of preeminent objective in European continent cannot be overemphasized. Intense, sustained, self-sacrificing efforts aimed at rapid consolidation of American Community's recently initiated fate-laden transatlantic enterprise are urgent, imperative, highly meritorious. Praying for such demonstration of heroism as will outshine exploits illuminating pages of American Bahá'í history in continents of Western Hemisphere.

[March 24, 1947]

Participation in Second Seven Year Plan

[MESSAGE TO 1947 CONVENTION]

My heart is filled with delight, wonder, pride and gratitude in contemplation of the peace-time exploits, in both hemispheres, of the world community of the followers of the Faith of Bahá'u'lláh, triumphantly emerging from the crucible of global war and moving irresistibly into the second epoch of the Formative Age of the Bahá'í Dispensation.

The opening years of the second century of the Bahá'í Era, synchronizing with concluding stage of the memorable quarter-century elapsed since the termination of the Heroic Age of the Faith, have been distinguished by a compelling demonstration by the entire body of believers, headed by the valorous American Bahá'í Community, of solidarity, resolve and self-sacrifice as well as by a magnificent record of systematic, world-wide achievements.

The three years since the celebration of the Centenary have been characterized by a simultaneous process of internal consolidation and steady enlargement of the orbit of a fast-evolving Administrative Order.

These years witnessed, first, the astounding resurgence of a war-devastated Bahá'í community of Central Europe, the rehabilitation of the communities in Southeast Asia, the Pacific Islands and the Far East; second, the inauguration of a new Seven Year Plan by the American Bahá'í Community destined to culminate with the Centenary of the Birth of Bahá'u'lláh's Prophetic Mission, aiming at the formation of three national assemblies in Latin America and the Dominion of Canada, at completion of the holiest House of Worship in the Bahá'í world, and at the erection of the structure of the Administrative Order in ten sovereign states of the European continent; and third, the formulation by the British, the Indian and the Persian National Assemblies of Six Year, Four and One-Half Year, and Forty-Five Month Plans respectively, culminating with the Centenary of the Báb's Martyrdom and pledged to establish nineteen spiritual assemblies in the British Isles, double the number of assemblies in the Indian subcontinent, establish ninety-five new centers of the Faith in Persia, convert the groups in Bahrein, Mecca and Kabul into assemblies and plant the banner of the Faith in the Arabian territories of Yemen, Oman, Ahsa and Kuweit.

Moreover, the number of countries opened to the onsweeping Faith, and the number of languages in which its literature has been translated and printed, is now raised to eighty-three and forty-seven, respectively. Four additional countries are in process of enrollment. Translations into fifteen other languages are being undertaken. No less than seventeen thousand pounds have accumulated for the international relief of war-afflicted Bahá'í communities of East and West. The Bahá'í endowments on the North American continent have now passed the two million dollar mark. The value of the endowments recently acquired at the World Center of the Faith, dedicated to the Shrines, are estimated at thirty-five thousand pounds. Bahá'í literature has been disseminated as far north as Upernavik, Greenland, above the Arctic Circle. The Bahá'í message has been broadcast by radio as far south as Magallanes. The area of land dedicated to the Mashriqu'l Adhkár of Persia has increased by almost a quarter-million square meters. The number of localities in the Antipodes where Bahá'ís reside has been raised to thirty-five, spread over Australia, New Zealand and Tasmania. Twenty-seven assemblies are functioning in Latin America. In over a hundred localities Bahá'ís are resident in Central and South America, almost double the localities at opening of the first Seven Year Plan. Historic Latin American conferences have been held in Buenos Aires and Panama. Summer schools are established in Argentina and Chile. Land has been offered in Chile for site of the first Mashriqu'l-Adhkár of Latin America. Additional assemblies have been incorporated in Paraguay and Colombia. Seven others are in process of incorporation. A notable impetus has been lent this world-redeeming Message through the concerted measures devised by the American National Assembly designed to proclaim the Faith to the masses through public conferences, press and radio.

Such remarkable multiplication of dynamic institutions, such thrilling deployment of world-regenerating forces, North, South, East and West, endow the preeminent goal of the Second Seven Year Plan in Europe with extraordinary urgency and peculiar significance. I am impelled to appeal to all American believers possessing independent means to arise and supplement the course of the second year of the Second Seven Year Plan through personal participation or appointment of deputies, the superb exertions of the heroic vanguard of the hosts destined, through successive decades, to achieve the spiritual conquest of the continent unconquered by Islám, rightly regarded as the mother of Christendom, the fountainhead of American culture, the mainspring of western civilization, and the recipient of the unique honor of two successive visits to its shores by the Center of Bahá'u'lláh's Covenant.

[April 28, 1947]

NSA Must Control Credentials of Foreigners

Owing to arrival of disloyal so-called Bahá'ís your Assembly's control of credentials should be strictly exercised, otherwise corruptive influences will spread and injure the magnificent services being achieved by the American Bahá'í Community.

[Circa June 1947]

The Challenging Requirements of the Present Hour

The opening years of the second century of the Bahá'í Era have synchronized with the termination of the first epoch of the Formative Age of the Bahá'í Dispensation, a Dispensation which posterity will recognize as the most glorious and momentous in the greatest cycle in the world's religious history.

The first seventy-seven years of the preceding century, constituting the Apostolic and Heroic Age of our Faith, fell into three distinct epochs, of nine, of thirty-nine and of twenty-nine years' duration, associated respectively with the Bábí Dispensation and the ministries of Bahá'u'lláh and of 'Abdu'l-Bahá. This Primitive Age of the Bahá'í Era, unapproached in spiritual fecundity by any period associated with the mission of the Founder of any previous Dispensation, was impregnated, from its inception to its termination, with the creative energies generated through the advent of two independent Manifestations and the establishment of a Covenant unique in the spiritual annals of mankind.

The last twenty-three years of that same century coincided with the first epoch of the second, the Iron and Formative, Age of the Dispensation of Bahá'u'lláh—the first of a series of epochs which must precede the inception of the last and Golden Age of that Dispensation—a Dispensation which, as the Author of the Faith has Himself categorically asserted, must extend over a period of no less than one thousand years, and which will constitute the first stage in a series of Dispensations, to be established by future Manifestations, all deriving their inspiration from the Author of the Bahá'í Revelation, and destined to last, in their aggregate, no less than five thousand centuries.

We are now entering the second epoch of the second Age of the first of these Dispensations. The first epoch witnessed the birth and the primary stages in the erection of the framework of the Administrative Order of the Faith—the nucleus and pattern of its World Order—according to the precepts laid down in 'Abdu'l-Bahá's Will and Testament, as well as the launching of the initial phase of the world-encompassing Plan bequeathed by Him to the American Bahá'í Community. That epoch was characterized by a twofold process aiming at the consolidation of the administrative structure of the Faith and the extension of the range of its institutions. It witnessed on the one hand, the emergence and the laying of the groundwork of that embryonic World Order whose advent was announced by the Báb in the Bayán, whose laws were revealed by Bahá'u'lláh in the Kitáb-i-Aqdas, and whose features were delineated by 'Abdu'l-Bahá in His Will and Testament. It was marked on the other hand by the launching, in the Western Hemisphere, of the first stage of a Plan whose original impulse was communicated by the Herald of our Faith in His Qayyúmu'l-Asmá', to whose implications the Author of the Bahá'í Revelation alluded in His Tablets, and whose Charter was revealed by the Center of His Covenant in the evening of His life.

The epoch we have now entered is destined to impart a great impetus to this historic, this twofold process. It must witness, on the one hand, the consummation of a laboriously constructed Administrative Order, and, on the other, the unfoldment of successive stages in the development of 'Abdu'l-Bahá's Plan beyond the confines of the Western Hemisphere and of the continent of Europe.

CROWNING FEATURE OF ADMINISTRATIVE ORDER: THE UNIVERSAL HOUSE OF JUSTICE

During this Formative Age of the Faith, and in the course of present and succeeding epochs, the last and crowning stage in the erection of the framework of the Administrative Order of the Faith of Bahá'u'lláh—the election of the Universal House of Justice—will have been completed, the Kitáb-i-Aqdas, the Mother-Book of His Revelation, will have been codified and its laws promulgated, the Lesser Peace will have been established, the unity of mankind will have been achieved and its maturity attained, the Plan conceived by 'Abdu'l-Bahá will have been executed, the emancipation of the Faith from the fetters of religious orthodoxy will have been effected, and its independent religious status will have been universally recognized, whilst in the course of the Golden Age, destined to consummate the Dispensation itself, the banner of the Most Great Peace, promised by its Author, will have been unfurled, the World Bahá'í Commonwealth will have emerged in the plenitude of its power and splendor, and the birth and efflorescence of a world civilization, the child of that Peace, will have conferred its inestimable blessings upon all mankind.

FOURFOLD OBJECTIVE TO PRESENT REQUIREMENTS

Not ours, however, to unriddle the workings of a distant future, or to dwell upon the promised glories of a God-impelled and unimaginably potent Revelation. Ours, rather, the task to cast our eyes upon, and bend our energies to meet, the challenging requirements of the present hour. Labors, of an urgent and sacred character, claim insistently our undivided attention during the opening years of this new epoch which we have entered. The Second Seven Year Plan, intended to carry a stage further the mission conceived by 'Abdu'l-Bahá for the American Bahá'í Community, is now entering its second year, and must, as it operates in three continents, be productive of results outshining any as yet achieved since the Divine Plan itself was set in motion during the concluding years of the first Bahá'í century. Unlike the plans which Bahá'í communities in Europe and on the Asiatic continent have spontaneously inaugurated since the commencement of the present century, the Plan with which the community of the "Apostles of Bahá'u'lláh" stands identified is divine in origin, is guided by the explicit and repeated instructions that have flowed from the pen of the Center of the Covenant Himself, is energized by the all-compelling will of its Author, claims as the theater for its operation territories spread over five continents and the islands of the seven seas, and must continue to function, ere its purpose is achieved, throughout successive epochs in the course of the Formative Age of the Bahá'í Dispensation. As it propels itself forward, driven by forces which its prosecutors can not hope to properly assess, as it spreads its ramifications to the furthest corners of the Western Hemisphere, and across the oceans to the continents of the Old World, and beyond them to the far-flung islands of the seas, this Plan, the birthright of the North American Bahá'í Community, will be increasingly regarded as an agency designed not only for the enlargement of the limits of the Faith and the multiplication of its institutions over the face of the planet, but for the acceleration of the construction and completion of the administrative framework of Bahá'u'lláh's embryonic World Order, hastening thereby the advent of that Golden Age which must witness the proclamation of the Most Great Peace and the unfoldment of that world civilization which is the offspring and primary purpose of that Peace.

The fourfold objective, which the prosecutors of the Plan, in the present early stage of its development, are now pursuing, and which is designed to stimulate the dual process initiated during the opening phase of the Formative Age of the Faith, must be strenuously and unfalteringly pursued. The second year of the Second Seven Year Plan must witness, on all fronts, on the part of young and old alike, rich and poor, colored and white, neophyte and veteran, a rededication to the tasks undertaken and an intensification of effort for their furtherance wholly unparalleled in the annals of American Bahá'í history. In every state of the United States, in every province of the Dominion of Canada, in every republic of Central and South America, in each of the ten selected sovereign states of the European continent, the ever-swelling legions of Bahá'u'lláh's steadily advancing army, obeying the Mandate of 'Abdu'l-Bahá, launched on the second stage of their world-wide crusade, deriving fresh courage from the exploits that have distinguished the opening phase of the present stage of their enterprise, must strain every nerve to scale loftier heights of heroism, and deploy, over a wider range, their divinely sustained forces, as their present Plan unfolds and moves towards a climax.

GOALS IN THE UNITED STATES AND ALASKA

In the United States of America, the base from which the manifold operations of this holy expedition are conducted, the enterprise associated with the completion of the first Mashriqu'l-Adhkár of the West, designed to consummate this historic undertaking in time for the celebration of its Jubilee in the year 1953, must be strenuously pushed forward. The prodigious efforts exerted for the erection of this noble edifice—the holiest House of Worship ever to be reared by the followers of Bahá'u'lláh—on which no less than one million four hundred thousand dollars have thus far been expended, and which will necessitate the expenditure of at least half a million more dollars, ere it is completed, must not, for one moment, be relaxed. The necessary modifications of the design chosen for its interior ornamentation should be adopted, the plans and specifications prepared, the preliminary contracts for its execution placed, and actual construction work started, if possible, ere the expiry of the present year.

The utmost effort by the National Teaching Committee and its auxiliary Regional Teaching Committees, aimed at raising the number of spiritual assemblies in the North American continent to no less than one hundred and seventy-five, ere the expiry of the current year, should be exerted. The eighty cities newly opened to the Faith should, likewise, be reinforced. The two hundred and eighteen groups already constituted should be continually encouraged to evolve into assemblies, while the vast number of localities, totalling over nine hundred, where isolated believers reside, should, however tremendous the exertion required, be enabled to attain group status, and be eventually converted into properly functioning assemblies.

Collateral to this process of reinforcing the fabrics of the Administrative Order and of widening its basis, a resolute attempt should be made by the national elected representatives of the entire community, aided by their Public Relations, Race Unity, Public Meetings, Visual

Education, College Speakers Bureau and Radio Committees, to reinforce the measures already adopted for the proclamation, through the press and radio, of the verities of the Faith to the masses, and for the establishment of closer contact with the leaders of public thought, with colleges and universities and with newspaper and magazine editors. National advertising and publicity should be further developed, the contact with seven hundred and fifty newspapers, magazines and trade papers should be maintained and the public relations programs amplified. Association, as distinct from affiliation, and untainted by any participation in political matters, with the various organs, leaders and representatives of the United Nations and kindred organizations should be stimulated for the purpose of giving, on the one hand, greater publicity to the aims and purposes of the Faith, and of paving the way, on the other, for the eventual conversion of a selected number of capable and receptive souls who will reinforce the ranks of its active and unreserved supporters.

The process of the incorporation of properly functioning spiritual assemblies must be simultaneously and vigorously carried out. The forty-five assemblies now incorporated are the first fruits of an enterprise of great significance, which must rapidly develop in the days to come, as an essential preliminary to the establishment, and the extension of the scope, of Bahá'í local endowments, as soon as the financial obligations incurred in connection with the completion of the Temple have been discharged. The institutions of the three summer schools, at Green Acre, Davison and Geyserville, and the International School at Temerity Ranch, as well as the activities of the Bahá'í Youth, must, under the close supervision of their respective national committees, be continually expanded and increasingly utilized as agencies for the furtherance of the vital objectives of the Plan.

The beneficial and highly responsible activities undertaken by the Publishing, the Reviewing, the Library, the Service for the Blind, the Visual Education, the Pamphlet Literature and Study Aids Committees, designed to disseminate and insure the integrity of Bahá'í literature, should, however indirectly connected with the purposes of the Plan, and within the limits imposed upon them through its operation, be steadily expanded, consolidated and be made to promote, in whatever way possible, its paramount interests.

Nor should the "spacious territory of Alaska," particularly mentioned by 'Abdu'l-Bahá in His Tablets of the Divine Plan, and at present the northern outpost of the Faith in the Western Hemisphere, be ignored, or its vital requirements neglected. The maintenance and consolidation of the first historic spiritual assembly in Anchorage, the northernmost administrative center of the Faith of Bahá'u'lláh in the world; the multiplication of Bahá'í centers in that territory; the propagation of the teachings among the Eskimos, emphasized by 'Abdu'l-Bahá's pen in those same Tablets; the translation and publication of selected passages from Bahá'í literature in their native language; the extension of the limits of the Faith beyond Fairbanks and nearer to the Arctic Circle—these constitute the urgent tasks facing the prosecutors of the present Plan in the years immediately ahead.

"Alaska is a vast country," are 'Abdu'l-Bahá's own words, recorded in those Tablets, ". . . Perchance, God willing, the lights of the Most Great Guidance will illuminate that country, and the breezes of the rose garden of the love of God will perfume the nostrils of the inhabitants of Alaska. Should you be aided to render such a service, rest ye assured that your heads shall be crowned with the diadem of everlasting sovereignty."

Canada to Form Separate National Assembly

In the Dominion of Canada, to whose significance and future the Author of the Tablets of the Divine Plan has repeatedly referred, and in all the nine provinces of which, as a direct result of the operation of the first Seven Year Plan, the Faith has established its spiritual assemblies, the Canadian believers, as a token of their recognition of the significance of the forthcoming formation of their first National Spiritual Assembly, must arise and carry out befittingly the task allotted to them in their homeland. Irrespective of the smallness of their numbers, notwithstanding the vastness of the territory for which they have been made responsible, and as a sign of their appreciation of the great bounty and independent status soon to be conferred upon them, they must, unitedly, exert a supreme effort to enlarge the limits, multiply the administrative centers, consolidate the institutions, and broadcast the truths and essentials of their beloved Faith throughout the length and breadth of that immense dominion.

The thirteen Canadian assemblies already formed should be, at all costs, maintained and fortified. The fifty-six localities where Bahá'ís reside should receive immediate attention, and the most promising among them should be chosen for the establishment of future assemblies, in order to broaden the basis and reinforce the foundations of the future pillar of the Universal House of Justice. Particular attention should, moreover, be paid to the need for the establishment, without delay, of the first Canadian Bahá'í summer school, which, as the scope of the activities of the Canadian believers extends, will have to be gradually supplemented by other institutions of a similar character, as has been the case in the development of summer schools in the United States of America. Preliminary steps should, likewise, be taken for the incorporation of all firmly grounded spiritual assemblies, as a prelude to the establishment of local and national endowments. The institution of the local Fund, in every center where the administrative structure of the Faith has been erected, should be assiduously developed. The holding of conferences designed to foster the unity, the solidarity and harmonious development of the Canadian Bahá'í Community should be steadily encouraged. An organized attempt should be made to broadcast the Message to the masses and their leaders through the medium of the press and radio. A deliberate and sustained endeavor should be exerted to win fresh recruits for the Faith from the ranks of the considerable French-speaking population of that dominion. The greatest care should be exercised to attract the attention, and win the support of other minorities in that land, such as the Indians, the Eskimos, the Dukhobors and the Negroes, thereby reinforcing the representative character of a rapidly developing community.

Nor should that community, as its local centers multiply, and the fabric of its national institutions is erected, and its maturity is demonstrated, and its independence vindicated, lose sight of, or neglect, the weighty provisions of those Tablets of the Divine Plan, addressed specifically to its members by 'Abdu'l-Bahá, wherein He confers upon them the mission of carrying the Message of His Father to territories and islands beyond the confines of that dominion, to Newfoundland and the Franklin Islands, to the Yukon, to Mackenzie, Keewatin, Ungava and Greenland. The tentative steps recently taken by a Danish believer in disseminating Bahá'í literature in the territory of Greenland, in a number of settlements and outposts beyond the Arctic Circle, and in dispatching Bahá'í books to Godthaab, its capital, and as far north as Upernavik on Baffin Bay, constitutes a modest yet historic beginning which the Canadian believers, in the light of 'Abdu'l-Bahá's Tablets addressed to them, must follow up in the years to come.

"Should the fire of the love of God be kindled in Greenland," He significantly assures them in one of the Tablets of the Divine Plan, "all the ice of that country will be melted, and its cold weather become temperate—that is, if the hearts be touched with the heat of the love of God, that territory will become a divine rose garden and a heavenly paradise, and the souls, even as fruitful trees, will acquire the utmost freshness and beauty. Effort, the utmost effort, is required."

Theirs is the duty, the privilege and honor, once their central administrative institution is firmly established, its subsidiary agencies are vigorously operating, and its immediate requirements are met, to take preliminary measures, on however small a scale, ere the Second Seven Year Plan is terminated, for the dispatch of a handful of pioneers to some of these territories, as an evidence of the determination and capacity of a newly independent national community to assume the functions, and discharge the responsibilities with which it has been invested in those immortal Tablets by the pen of the Center of Bahá'u'lláh's Covenant.

"There is no difference between countries," is 'Abdu'l-Bahá's testimony in one of those Tablets. "The future of the Dominion of Canada, however, is very great, and the events connected with it infinitely glorious. It shall become the object of the glance of Providence, and shall show forth the bounties of the All-Glorious." "Again I repeat," He, in that same Tablet affirms, "that the future of Canada is very great, whether from a material or a spiritual standpoint. . . . The clouds of the Kingdom will water the seeds of guidance which have been sown there."

TASKS IN LATIN AMERICA

In the far-flung Latin American field, where the first fruits of the Divine Plan, operating beyond the confines of the North American continent, have already been garnered in such abundance, the Latin American Bahá'í communities, from the Mexican border to the extremity of Chile, should bestir themselves for the collective, the historic and gigantic tasks that await them, and which must culminate, ere the expiry of the present Plan, in the formation of two national spiritual assemblies for Central and South America.

The marvelous progress achieved as a result of the operation of the first Seven Year Plan, as evidenced by the establishment of full-fledged spiritual assemblies in the virgin territories of no less than fourteen republics, and the formation of active groups in the remaining republics, has been enhanced by the even more startling expansion of Bahá'í activity since the termination of the first stage of the Divine Plan. As a result of this expansion spiritual assemblies have been established in all the remaining republics, the number of localities where Bahá'ís reside has been raised to over a hundred, almost double the number of localities in which the Faith had been introduced after the completion of the first Seven Year Plan, the number of spiritual assemblies has swelled to no less than thirty-seven, three of which have been duly incorporated, a notable impetus has been given to the activities of the distributing centers of Bahá'í literature in Argentina and Panama, historic conferences have been held in these two republics, summer schools have been inaugurated in Argentina and Chile, and a tract of land has been presented as a site for the first Mashriqu'l-Adhkár in Latin America. No community since the inception of the hundred-year-old Faith of Bahá'u'lláh, not even the community of the Most Great Name in the North American continent, can boast of an evolution as rapid, a consolidation as sound, a multiplication of centers as swift, as those that have marked the birth and rise of the community of His followers in Latin America.

The colossal tasks that now summon this Latin American Bahá'í community to a challenge, cannot but dwarf, if faithfully and promptly accomplished, the magnificent achievements that have immortalized the first decade of organized activity in Latin American Bahá'í history. The seed-sowing stage associated, in the main, with the labors and travels of that saintly soul, that star-servant of the Faith of Bahá'u'lláh, the incomparable Martha Root, links this decade of organized Bahá'í activity in Latin America with both the closing years of the Heroic Age of our Faith and the first fifteen years of the initial epoch of the Age we live in.

Two Regional National Assemblies a Vital Objective

The emergence of organized local communities in most of the republics of Latin America will be forever associated with the exploits that have shed such luster on the first stage of the Divine Plan launched during the concluding years of that first epoch of the Formative Age of our Faith. The constitution of two independent duly elected national spiritual assemblies for the northern and southern zones of Latin America is now to be regarded as one of the most vital objectives of the Second Seven Year Plan, whose inauguration synchronizes with the opening years of the second Bahá'í century, and which will be chiefly associated with the first phase of the second epoch of that Age. The emergence of these two national assemblies, precursors of the institutions which must participate in the election, and contribute to the support, of the Universal House of Justice—the last crowning unit in the erection of the fabric of the Administrative Order of the Faith of Bahá'u'lláh—must lead gradually and uninterruptedly, and in the course of successive epochs of the Formative Age, to the constitution in each of the republics of Central and South America, of a properly elected, fully representative national assembly, constituting thereby the last stage in the administrative evolution of that Faith throughout Latin America.

In order that these future tasks may be carried out with dispatch, efficiency, harmony and in strict accordance with the administrative and spiritual principles of our Faith, the Latin American promoters of the present Seven Year Plan must focus their attention on the requirements of the present hour, close their ranks, reinforce the bonds of unity, of solidarity and of cooperation which unite them, rededicate themselves individually to the sacred, all-important and vital task of teaching, exert strenuous endeavors to deepen their knowledge of the history and fundamentals of their Faith, steep themselves in the spirit and the love of its teachings and acquire special training for future pioneer activity throughout the length and breadth of the vast stretches of territory which extend from the confines of the great republic in the north to the Straits of Magellan in the south.

The process of the steady multiplication of spiritual assemblies, already numbering thirty-seven, of groups whose number equals that of the assemblies, and of the forty localities where isolated believers reside, must vigorously and uninterruptedly continue. The incorporation of well-grounded spiritual assemblies, following the example set by the spiritual assemblies of San José, Costa Rica, of Bogotá, Colombia, and of Asunción, Paraguay, as a preliminary to the incorporation of the future national assemblies to be established in Latin America, must be strenuously and efficiently carried out. A beginning, however modest, should be made in the direction of establishing local Funds, supported by native believers and designed to supplement the financial assistance extended by the parent community in North America, for the further-ance of pioneer activity, for the dissemination of Bahá'í literature, for the maintenance of local Bahá'í headquarters, for the gradual initiation of Bahá'í endowments, such as the land offered for a Bahá'í Temple in Chile, for the holding of conferences and of summer schools, for the creation of publicity agencies, and for the conduct and expansion of youth activities.

Strong and sustained support should be given to the vitally needed and meritorious activities started by the native Latin American travel-ing teachers, particularly in the pioneer field, who, as the mighty task progresses, must increasingly bear the brunt of responsibility for the propagation of the Faith in their homelands. Full advantage should be taken of the facilities provided by the use of practical workshop courses in Latin American pioneering at the International School at Temerity Ranch. The two summer schools in Azeiza and Santiago, as well as one planned in Vera Cruz, should be utilized, not only as centers for the acquisition of Bahá'í learning, but as training grounds for pioneering among the Spanish and Portuguese speaking populations of all the republics of Latin America. The regional conferences held in Buenos Aires and Panama should be followed by conferences of a similar character, at which a growing number of attendants from among the ranks of Latin American believers will assume an ever-increasing share of responsibility in the initiation and conduct of the affairs of a continually evolving community. A deliberate effort should be made to increase, through correspondence teaching and its extension to all the Spanish speaking countries, the number of the active supporters of the Faith, so desperately needed in view of the vastness of the field, the mighty responsibilities that have been incurred, the smallness of the number of laborers, and the shortness of the time at their disposal.

Other agencies, such as publicity and advertising in the press, the multiplication of accurate and improved radio scripts, the extension of teaching projects through regional teaching committees, visual educa-tion and the organization of public meetings, should be fully utilized to capture the attention, win the sympathy, and secure the active and unreserved support of a steadily increasing proportion of the population of the various Latin American republics. The publishing activities of a constantly growing community should, likewise, be stimulated, their scope should be continually widened, the quality of Bahá'í publications in Spanish, Portuguese and French be improved, and their dissemination over a wide area be insured. The two Spanish bulletins, the one already published in Santiago and the other planned in San José, should, likewise, as an adjunct to Bahá'í publications, be developed and widely circulated. The contact established with the two hundred and forty-four Masonic Lodges should be reinforced by similar contacts with schools as well as business firms established throughout the various republics, for the sole purpose of giving further publicity to the Faith, and winning ultimately fresh recruits to the strength of its followers.

IMPORTANCE OF THE AMERICAN INDIANS

Particular attention, I feel, should, at this juncture, be directed to the various Indian tribes, the aboriginal inhabitants of the Latin republics, whom the Author of the Tablets of the Divine Plan has compared to the "ancient inhabitants of the Arabian Peninsula." "Attach great importance," is His admonition to the entire body of the believers in the United States and the Dominion of Canada, "to the indigenous population of America. For these souls may be likened unto the ancient inhabitants of the Arabian Peninsula, who, prior to the Mission of Muḥammad, were like unto savages. When the light of Muḥammad shone forth in their midst, however, they became so radiant as to illumine the world. Likewise, these Indians, should they be educated and guided, there can be no doubt that they will become so illumined as to enlighten the whole world." The initial contact already established, in the concluding years of the first Bahá'í century, in obedience to 'Abdu'l-Baha's Mandate, with the Cherokee and Oneida Indians in North Carolina and Wisconsin, with the Patagonian, the Mexican and the Inca Indians, and the Mayans in Argentina, Mexico, Peru and Yucatan, respectively, should, as the Latin American Bahá'í communities gain in stature and strength, be consolidated and extended. A special effort should be exerted to secure the unqualified adherence of members of some of these tribes to the Faith, their subsequent election to its councils, and their unreserved support of the organized attempts that will have to be made in the future by the projected national assemblies for the large-scale conversion of Indian races to the Faith of Bahá'u'lláh.

Nor should the peculiar position of the Republic of Panama be overlooked at the present stage in the development of the Faith in Latin America. "All the above countries," 'Abdu'l-Bahá, referring to the Central American republics in one of the Tablets of His Divine Plan, has affirmed, "have importance, but especially the Republic of Panama, wherein the Atlantic and Pacific Oceans come together through the Panama Canal. It is a center for travel and passage from America to other continents of the world, and in the future it will gain most great importance." "Likewise," He moreover has written, "ye must give great attention to the Republic of Panama, for in that point the Occident and the Orient find each other united through the Panama Canal, and it is also situated between the two great oceans. That place will become very important in the future. The teachings, once established there, will unite the East and the West, the North and the South."

The manifold activities initiated since the launching of the first Seven Year Plan should, under no circumstances, be neglected or allowed to stagnate. The excellent publicity accorded the Faith, and the contact established with several leaders in that republic should be followed up, systematically and with the greatest care, by the growing community within its confines. The initial contact with the Indians should be developed with assiduous care and unfailing patience. Furthermore, the strengthening of the bonds now being forged between the North American communities and their sister communities in Latin America must constitute, owing to the unique and central position occupied by that republic, one of the chief objectives of the Panamanian believers, the progress of whose activities deserves to rank as one of the most notable chapters of recent Latin American Bahá'í history.

Nor should the valuable and meritorious labors accomplished since the inception of the first Seven Year Plan in Punta Arenas de Magallanes, that far-off center situated not only on the southern extremity of the Western Hemisphere, but constituting the southernmost outpost of the Faith in the whole world, be for a moment neglected in the course of the second stage in the development of the Divine Plan. The assembly already constituted in that city, the remarkable radio publicity secured by the believers there, the assistance extended by them to the teaching work in other parts of Chile, should be regarded only as a prelude to the work of consolidation which must be indefatigably pursued. This work, if properly carried out, in conjunction with the activities associated with the assemblies of Santiago, Valparaíso and Viña del Mar, and the groups of Puerto Montt, Valdivia, Quilpue, Temuco, Sewell, Chorrillos, Mulchén and other smaller ones, as well as several isolated localities in that republic, may well hasten the advent of the day when the Chilean followers of the Faith of Bahá'u'lláh will have established the first independent national spiritual assembly to be formed by any single nation of Latin America.

Bahá'u'lláh's Summons to the Western Hemisphere

Whoever it may be among these Latin American communities who will eventually carry off the palm of victory, and win this immortal distinction, all without exception, and with equal zeal, must participate in this vast and collective enterprise which is engaging, in an ever-increasing measure, their attention and challenging their resources. Let them remember that the Author of their Faith has in His Kitáb-i-Aqdas, the Mother-Book of His Revelation, singled out the company of the Presidents of their countries, together with those of the North American continent, and addressed them in terms that sharply contrast with the dire warnings and condemnatory words addressed directly and indirectly, to the King of Prussia, the French and Austrian Emperors and the Sultan of Turkey, who, together with those Presidents, are the only sovereigns and rulers specifically mentioned by Him in that Book.

"Hearken ye, O rulers of America and the Presidents of the Republics therein!" is His summons sounded in that mighty Charter of the future world civilization, "unto that which the Dove is warbling on the Branch of Eternity: There is none other God but Me, the Ever-Abiding, the Forgiving, the All-Bountiful. Adorn ye the temple of dominion with the ornament of justice and of the fear of God, and its head with the crown of the remembrance of your Lord, the Creator of the heavens. Thus counselleth you He Who is the Dayspring of Names, as bidden by Him Who is the All-Knowing, the All-Wise. The Promised One hath appeared in this glorified Station, whereat all beings, both seen and unseen, have rejoiced. Take ye advantage of the Day of God. Verily, to meet Him is better for you than all that whereon the sun shineth, could ye but know it. O concourse of rulers! Give ear unto that which hath been raised from the Dayspring of Grandeur: Verily, there is none other God but Me, the Lord of Utterance, the All-Knowing. Bind ye the broken with the hands of justice, and crush the oppressor who flourisheth with the rod of the commandments of your Lord, the Ordainer, the All-Wise."

Let them ponder the honor which the Author of the Revelation Himself has chosen to confer upon their countries, the obligations which that honor automatically brings in its wake, the opportunities it offers, the power it releases for the removal of all obstacles, however formidable, which may be encountered in their path, and the promise of guidance it implies for the attainment of the objectives alluded to in these memorable passages.

To the eager, the warm-hearted, the spiritually minded and staunch members of these Latin American Bahá'í communities who, among the followers of Bahá'u'lláh, already constitute the most considerable body of recruits from the ranks of the most deeply entrenched and powerful Church of Christendom; whose motherlands have been chosen as the scene of the earliest victories won by the prosecutors of 'Abdu'l-Bahá's Divine Plan; launched on their crusade for the spiritual conquest of the whole planet; the establishment of whose projected national spiritual assemblies must constitute a notable landmark in the second epoch of the Formative Age of the Bahá'í Dispensation; whose leading spiritual assemblies are now establishing direct contact with the World Center of the Faith of Bahá'u'lláh in the Holy Land; the photographs of whose elected representatives, at their chief centers, will soon adorn the walls of His Mansion at Bahjí; a few of whose members have already arisen to carry back the torch of divine guidance entrusted to their care to the peoples and races from which they have sprung—to this privileged, this youngest, this dynamic and highly promising member of the organic Bahá'í World Community, I feel moved, before I dismiss this aspect of my theme, to direct this general appeal to rise to the heights of the glorious opportunity which destiny is unfolding before its members. Theirs is the opportunity, if they but seize it, to adorn the opening pages of the annals of the second Bahá'í century with a tale of deeds approaching in valor those with which their Persian brethren have illuminated the opening years of the first, and comparable with the exploits more recently achieved by their North American fellow-believers and which have shed such luster on the closing decade of that same century.

SPIRITUAL CRUSADE TO BE LAUNCHED IN EUROPE

To the fourth, and by far the most momentous, the most arduous, the most challenging task to be carried out under the Second Seven Year Plan—the systematic launching of a crusade in a mighty, a tormented, a spiritually famished continent, a continent drawn, in recent years through political developments as well as through improvement in the means of transportation, so close to the great republic of the West, and constituting a stepping-stone on the road leading to the redemption of the Old World—I must now direct the attention of my readers.

This as yet unfought and unbelievably potent crusade, embarked upon in the opening decade of the second century of the Bahá'í Era, signalizing the commencement of the second epoch of the Formative Age of the Dispensation of Bahá'u'lláh, and marking the first stage in the propulsion of a divinely conceived Plan across the borders of the Western Hemisphere, must, as its pace augments, reveal the first signs and tokens which, as anticipated by the Author of the Plan Himself, must accompany the carrying of His Father's Message across the ocean, at the hands of His "apostles," from the shores of their homeland to the European continent. "The moment," is His powerfully sustaining, gloriously inspiring promise, "this Divine Message is carried forward by the American believers from the shores of America, and is propagated through the continents of Europe, of Asia, of Africa and of Australia, and as far as the islands of the Pacific, this community will find itself securely established upon the throne of an everlasting dominion. Then will all the peoples of the world witness that this community is spiritually illumined and divinely guided. Then will the whole earth resound with the praises of its majesty and greatness."

The first stage in this transatlantic field of service which those crusading for the Cause of Bahá'u'lláh in the Western Hemisphere are now entering is a step fraught with possibilities such as no mind can adequately envisage. Its challenge is overwhelming and its potentialities unfathomable. Its hazards, rigors and pitfalls are numerous, its field immense, the number of its promoters as yet utterly inadequate, the resources required for its effective prosecution barely tapped. The races, nations and classes included within its orbit are numerous and highly diversified, and the prizes to be won by its victors incalculably great. The hatreds that inflame, the rivalries that agitate, the controversies that confuse, the miseries that afflict, these races, nations and classes are bitter and of long standing. The influence and fanaticism, whether ecclesiastical or political, of potentially hostile organizations, firmly entrenched within their ancestral strongholds, are formidable.

The members of the North American Bahá'í Community, to whose care the immediate destinies of this fate-laden crusade have been entrusted, are standing at a new crossroads. Behind them is an imperishable record, brief yet illustrious, of feats performed over the entire range of the Western Hemisphere. Before them stretches a vista alluring in its as yet hazy outlines, entrancing in its magnitude, reaching to the far horizons of as yet unconquered territories. They can look back, since that crusade was launched, upon a decade of modest beginnings, of toilsome labors, of richly deserved rewards. They now look forward to successive epochs reaching as far as the fringes of that Golden Age that is to be, glowing in the light of God-given promises, destined to be traversed at the cost of infinite toil and of heroic self-sacrifice.

They can neither retrace their steps, nor falter, nor even afford to mark time. The sands are running out, the short span of six brief years intervening between the present hour and the termination of the second stage of the enterprise on which they have embarked will soon expire. The hosts on high, having sounded the signal, are impatient to rush forward, and demonstrate anew the irresistible force of their might. Europe, in the throes of the aftermath of a horribly devastating conflict, calls desperately, in one of the darkest hours of its history, for that sovereign remedy which only the Plan, conceived by a divinely appointed Physician, can administer. Sister communities, in the north and in the heart of that continent, alive to the needs, the opportunities and the glorious mission of the vanguard of Bahá'u'lláh's crusaders, now landing on the shores of that agitated continent, are only too eager to reinforce the stupendous exertions that must needs be made for its ultimate redemption. Nor will other sister communities further afield refrain, for a moment, from lending a helping hand, once the progress of this gigantic movement now set in motion is accelerated. Above and beyond them all, unsleeping, ever-solicitous, unerring, is the Pilot of their bark, the Charterer of their course, the Founder of their spiritual fellowship, the Bestower of that primacy which is the hallmark of their destiny.

EVOLVING STRONGHOLDS IN TEN INITIAL COUNTRIES

The ten countries, constituting the initial field wherein the prowess of these crusaders must, in the years immediately ahead, be exhibited, and in whose capitals the foundations of the embryonic Order of the Faith of Bahá'u'lláh must preferably be unassailably laid, must each evolve into strongholds from which the dynamic energies of that Faith can be diffused to neighboring territories in the course of the unfoldment of the Plan. The nuclei that are now being formed, and the groups that are beginning to emerge, must be speedily and systematically reinforced, not only through the dispatch and settlement of pioneers and the visits paid them by itinerant teachers, but also through the progressive development of the teaching work which the pioneers themselves must initiate and foster among the native population in those countries. Any artificially created assembly, consisting of settlers from abroad, can at best be considered as temporary and insecure, and should, if the second stage of the European enterprise is to be commenced without undue delay in the future, be supplanted by broadbased, securely grounded, efficiently functioning assemblies, composed primarily of the people of the countries themselves, who are firm in faith, unimpeachable in their loyalty and whole-hearted in their support of the Administrative Order of the Faith. The twenty-five pioneers that have already proceeded to Scandinavia and the Low Countries, to the Iberian Peninsula, to Switzerland and Italy, should, in the course of this current year, and while the process of teaching the native population is being inaugurated, be reinforced by as many additional pioneers as possible, and particularly by those who, possessed of independent means, can, either themselves or through their appointed deputies, swell the number of the valiant workers already laboring with such devotion in those fields.

The translation, the publication and dissemination of Bahá'í literature, whether in the form of leaflets, pamphlets or books, in the nine selected languages, should, as the work progresses and the demand is correspondingly increased, be strenuously carried out, as a preliminary to its free distribution among the public on certain occasions, and its presentation to both the leaders of public thought and the numerous and famous libraries established in those countries. No time should be lost in establishing, on however small a scale, initial contact with the press and other agencies designed to invite greater attention on the part of the masses to the historic work now being initiated in their respective countries.

No opportunity, in view of the necessity of insuring the harmonious development of the Faith, should be ignored, which its potential enemies, whether ecclesiastical or otherwise, may offer, to set forth, in a restrained and unprovocative language, its aims and tenets, to defend its interests, to proclaim its universality, to assert the supernatural, the supra-national and non-political character of its institutions, and its acceptance of the divine origin of the Faiths which have preceded it. Nor should any chance be missed of associating the Faith, as distinct from affiliating it, with all progressive, non-political, non-ecclesiastical institutions, whether social, educational, or charitable, whose objectives harmonize with some of its tenets, and amongst whose members and supporters individuals may be found who will eventually embrace its truth. Particular attention should, moreover, be paid to attendance at congresses and conferences, and to any contacts that can be made with colleges and universities which offer a fertile field for the scattering of the seeds of the Faith, and afford opportunities for broadcasting its message, and for winning fresh recruits to its strength.

Nor should any occasion be neglected by the pioneers of attending, if their personal circumstances permit, either the British or German Bahá'í summer schools, and of forging such links with these institutions as will not only assist them in the discharge of their duties, but enable them to initiate, when the time is ripe, an institution of a similar character, under the auspices of the European Teaching Committee —an institution which will be the forerunner of the summer schools that will have to be founded separately by the future assemblies in their respective countries. Above all, any assistance which the two national spiritual assemblies, already established on that continent, and their auxiliary committees, and particularly their publishing agencies, can extend should be gratefully welcomed and utilized to the full, until such time as the institutions destined to evolve in these countries can assume independently the conduct of their own affairs.

A constant interchange of news between the centers, through the medium of the Geneva Bulletin, whose scope must be steadily enlarged, and close contact with each other through the European office of the European Teaching Committee, functioning as an adjunct to the International Bahá'í Bureau, should, furthermore, be maintained and reinforced, whenever circumstances are favorable, by the convening of conferences, which will bring together as many pioneers laboring in these ten countries, and newly converted believers, as possible, enabling them to jointly consider their plans, problems and activities, concert measures for the progress of the Faith in that continent, and pave the way for the future formation of regional national spiritual assemblies, which must precede the constitution of separate independent national institutions in each of these countries. Such summer schools and conferences, initiated and conducted by one of the most important agencies of the highest administrative institution in the North American Bahá'í Community, gathering together as they will Bahá'í representatives of various races and nations on the continent of Europe, will, by reason of their unprecedented character in the evolution of the Faith, since its inception, constitute a historic landmark in the development of the organic world-wide Bahá'í community, and will be the harbinger of those epoch-making world conferences, at which the representatives of the nations and races within the Bahá'í fold will convene for the strengthening of the spiritual and administrative bonds that unite its members.

INITIATING NATIONAL HEADQUARTERS AND ADAPTING TEACHING METHODS

A beginning, however limited in scope, should be made, ere the present stage of the Divine Plan draws to a close, in the direction of establishing befitting administrative headquarters for the rising communities and their projected assemblies in the capital cities of Stockholm, of Oslo, of Copenhagen, of The Hague, of Brussels, of Luxembourg, of Madrid, of Lisbon, of Rome and of Bern, through the rental of suitable quarters which, in the course of time, must lead to either the construction or the purchase in each of these capitals of a national Ḥaẓíratu'l-Quds, as a future seat for independent, elected national spiritual assemblies.

A tentative start, though strictly speaking excluded from the scope of the present Plan, should, I feel, be made, ere the six remaining years have run their course, aiming at the formation, in each of the ten designated countries, of a number of nuclei, however few, however unstable, which will proclaim to the entire Bahá'í world the ability of the prosecutors of the Plan to exceed their allocated task, even as they surpassed, in the Latin American field, the goals which they had originally set before them. Such a feat, if accomplished, would impart to my overburdened heart a joy that would equal the many consolations which a dearly loved community has showered upon me, in the past, by its signal acts, both within its homeland and abroad, since the passing of 'Abdu'l-Bahá.

Nor should any of the pioneers, at this early stage in the upbuilding of Bahá'í national communities, overlook the fundamental prerequisite for any successful teaching enterprise, which is to adapt the presentation of the fundamental principles of their Faith to the cultural and religious backgrounds, the ideologies, and the temperament of the divers races and nations whom they are called upon to enlighten and attract. The susceptibilities of these races and nations, from both the northern and southern climes, springing from either the Germanic or Latin stock, belonging to either the Catholic or Protestant communion, some democratic, others totalitarian in outlook, some socialistic, others capitalistic in their tendencies, differing widely in their customs and standards of living, should at all times be carefully considered, and under no circumstances neglected.

These pioneers, in their contact with the members of divers creeds, races and nations, covering a range which offers no parallel in either the north or south continents, must neither antagonize them nor compromise with their own essential principles. They must be neither provocative nor supine, neither fanatical nor excessively liberal, in their exposition of the fundamental and distinguishing features of their Faith. They must be either wary or bold, they must act swiftly or mark time, they must use the direct or indirect method, they must be challenging or conciliatory, in strict accordance with the spiritual receptivity of the soul with whom they come in contact, whether he be a nobleman or a commoner, a northerner or a southerner, a layman or a priest, a capitalist or a socialist, a statesman or a prince, an artisan or a beggar. In their presentation of the Message of Bahá'u'lláh they must neither hesitate nor falter. They must be neither contemptuous of the poor nor timid before the great. In their exposition of its verities they must neither overstress nor whittle down the truth which they champion, whether their hearer belong to royalty, or be a prince of the church, or a politician, or a tradesman, or a man of the street. To all alike, high or low, rich or poor, they must proffer, with open hands, with a radiant heart, with an eloquent tongue, with infinite patience, with uncompromising loyalty, with great wisdom, with unshakable courage, the Cup of Salvation at so critical an hour, to the confused, the hungry, the distraught and fear-stricken multitudes, in the north, in the west, in the south and in the heart, of that sorely tried continent.

EUROPE FEELS STIRRINGS OF SPIRITUAL REVOLUTION

The second century of the Bahá'í Era has dawned. The second stage of the Divine Plan has been launched. The second epoch of the Formative Age of the Bahá'í Dispensation has opened. The tragedy of a continent, so blessed, so rich in history, so harassed, is moving towards a climax. The vanguard of the torchbearers of a world-redeeming civilization are landing on its shores and are settling in its capitals. An epoch has commenced, inaugurating the systematic conquest of the European continent by the organized body of the "apostles of Bahá'u'lláh," destined to unfold its potentialities in the course of succeeding centuries, and bidding fair to eclipse the radiance of those past ages which have successfully witnessed the introduction of the Christian Faith into the continent's northern climes, the efflorescence of Islamic culture that shed such radiance along its southern shores, and the rise of the Reformation in its very heart.

The stage is set. The hour is propitious. The signal is sounded. Bahá'u'lláh's spiritual battalions are moving into position. The initial clash between the forces of darkness and the army of light, as unnoticed as the landing, two milleniums ago, of the apostles of Christ on the southern shores of the European continent, is being registered by the denizens of the Abhá Kingdom. The Author of the Plan that has set so titanic an enterprise in motion is Himself mounted at the head of these battalions, and leads them on to capture the cities of men's hearts. A continent, twice blessed by 'Abdu'l-Bahá's successive visits to its shores, and the scene of His first public appearance in the West; which has been the cradle of a civilization to some of whose beneficent features the pen of Bahá'u'lláh has paid significant tribute; on whose soil both the

Greek and Roman civilizations were born and flourished; which has contributed so richly to the unfoldment of American civilization; the fountainhead of American culture; the mother of Christendom, and the scene of the greatest exploits of the followers of Jesus Christ; in some of whose outlying territories have been won some of the most resplendent victories which ushered in the Golden Age of Islám; which sustained, in its very heart, the violent impact of the onrushing hosts of that Faith, intent on the subjugation of its cities, but which refused to bend the knee to its invaders, and succeeded in the end in repulsing their assault—such a continent is now experiencing, at the hands of the little as yet unnoticed band of pioneers sent forth by the enviable, the privileged, the dynamic American Bahá'í Community, the first stirrings of that spiritual revolution which must culminate, in the Golden Age that is as yet unborn, in the permanent establishment of Bahá'u'lláh's Order throughout that continent.

Divine Plan Challenges North American Believers

One word in conclusion to those to whom the Tablets of so stupendous a Plan have been addressed, to whose care the destinies of so prodigious an enterprise have been committed, and of whom such titanic efforts are now demanded. I can do no better than recall, nor can I sufficiently emphasize, or refrain from quoting anew, those stirring and pregnant passages that illuminate the pages of 'Abdu'l-Bahá's epoch-making Tablets.

In one of these Tablets, addressed to the believers in the Northeastern States, these weighty and highly significant words are recorded: "All countries, in the estimation of the one true God, are but one country, and all cities and villages are on an equal footing . . . Through faith and certitude, and the precedence achieved by one over another, however, the dweller conferreth honor upon the dwelling, some of the countries achieve distinction, and attain a preeminent position. For instance, notwithstanding that some of the countries of Europe and of America are distinguished by, and surpass other countries in, the salubrity of their climate, the wholesomeness of their water, and the charm of their mountains, plains and prairies, yet Palestine became the glory of all nations inasmuch as all the holy and Divine Manifestations, from the time of Abraham until the appearance of the Seal of the Prophets (Muḥammad), have lived in, or migrated to, or traveled through, that country. Likewise, Mecca and Medina have achieved illimitable glory, as the light of Prophethood shone forth therein. For this reason Palestine and Ḥijáz have been distinguished from all other countries." "Likewise," is His remarkable disclosure, "the continent of America is, in the eyes of the one true God, the land wherein the splendors of His light shall be revealed, where the mysteries of His Faith shall be unveiled, the home of the righteous, and the gathering-place of the free."

To those of His followers, dwelling in that enviable and blessed continent, He has chosen to address these no less inspiring words, as recorded in one of those Tablets revealed in honor of the believers of the United States and Canada: "O ye apostles of Bahá'u'lláh! May my life be sacrificed for you! . . . Behold the portals which Bahá'u'lláh hath opened before you! Consider how exalted and lofty is the station you are destined to attain, how unique the favors with which you have been endowed . . . My thoughts are turned towards you, and my heart leaps within me at your mention. Could ye know how my soul gloweth with your love, so great a happiness would flood your hearts as to cause you to become enamored with each other." "The full measure of your success," He, in another Tablet, addressed to the entire company of His followers in the North American continent these prophetic words: "is as yet unrevealed, its significance unapprehended. Erelong ye will with your own eyes witness how brilliantly every one of you, even as a shining star, will radiate in the firmament of your country the light of divine guidance, and will bestow upon its people the glory of an everlasting life . . . I fervently hope that in the near future the whole earth may be stirred and shaken by the results of your achievements. The hope which 'Abdu'l-Bahá cherishes for you is that the same success which has attended your efforts in America may crown your endeavors in other parts of the world, that through you the fame of the Cause of God may be diffused throughout the East and the West, and the advent of the Kingdom of the Lord of Hosts be proclaimed in all the five continents of the globe. The moment this Divine Message is carried forward by the American believers from the shores of America, and is propagated through the continents of Europe, of Asia, of Africa and of Australia, and as far as the islands of the Pacific, this community will find itself securely established upon the throne of an everlasting dominion. Then will all the peoples of the world witness that this community is spiritually illumined and divinely guided. Then will the whole earth resound with the praises of its majesty and greatness . . . Know ye of a certainty that whatever gathering ye enter, the waves of the Holy Spirit are surging over it, and the heavenly grace of the Blessed Beauty encompasseth that gathering . . . O that I could travel, even though on foot and in the utmost poverty, to these regions, and, raising the call of Yá-Bahá'u'l-Abhá in cities, villages, mountains, deserts and oceans promote the divine teachings! This, alas, I cannot do. How intensely I deplore it! Please God, ye may achieve it . . . Thus far ye have been untiring in your labors. Let your exertions henceforth increase a thousandfold. Summon the people in these countries, capitals, islands, assemblies and churches to enter the Abhá Kingdom. The scope of your exertions must needs be extended. The wider its range, the more striking will be the evidence of divine assistance."

DETACHMENT FROM THE PHYSICAL WORLD

"Now is the time," He no less significantly remarks in another of these Tablets, "for you to divest yourselves of the garment of attachment to this world that perisheth, to be wholly severed from the physical world, become heavenly angels, and travel to these countries. I swear by Him besides Whom there is none other God that each one of you will become an Isráfíl of Life, and will blow the Breath of Life into the souls of others." And lastly this glorious promise in another of those immortal Tablets: "Should success crown your enterprise, America will assuredly evolve into a center from which waves of spiritual power will emanate, and the throne of the Kingdom of God, will, in the plenitude of its majesty and glory, be firmly established."

In one of the earliest Tablets addressed by Him to the American believers these equally significant words have been penned: "If ye be truly united, if ye agree to promote that which is the essential purpose, and to show forth an all-unifying love, I swear by Him Who causeth the seed to split and the breeze to waft, so great a light will shine forth from your faces as to reach the highest heavens, the fame of your glory will be noised abroad, the evidences of your preeminence will spread throughout all regions, your power will penetrate the realities of all things, your aims and purposes will exert their influence upon the great and mighty nations, your spirits will encompass the whole world of being, and ye will discover yourselves to be kings in the dominions of the Kingdom, and attired with the glorious crowns of the invisible Realm, and become the marshals of the army of peace, and princes of the forces of light, and stars shining from the horizon of perfection, and brilliant lamps shedding their radiance upon men."

CONTRIBUTION OF THE WEST TO WORLD ORDER

In the light of these glowing tributes, these ardent hopes, these soul-stirring promises, recorded by the pen of the Center of the Covenant, is it surprising to find that the Author of the Covenant Himself has, anticipating the great contribution which the West is destined to make to the establishment of His World Order, made such a momentous statement in His writings: "In the East the light of His Revelation hath broken; in the West have appeared the signs of His dominion. Ponder this in your hearts, O people, and be not of those who have turned a deaf ear to the admonitions of Him Who is the Almighty, the All-Praised."

'Abdu'l-Bahá Himself, confirming this statement, has written: "From the beginning of time until the present day the light of Divine Revelation hath risen in the East and shed its radiance upon the West. The illumination thus shed hath, however, acquired in the West an extraordinary brilliancy. Consider the Faith proclaimed by Jesus. Though it first appeared in the East, yet not until its light had been shed upon the West did the full measure of its potentialities become manifest." "The day is approaching when ye shall witness how, through the splendor of the Faith of Bahá'u'lláh the West will have replaced the East, radiating the light of divine guidance." "The West hath acquired illumination from the East, but, in some respects the reflection of the light hath been greater in the Occident." "The East hath, verily, been illumined with the light of the Kingdom. Erelong will this same light shed a still greater illumination through the potency of the teachings of God, and their souls be set aglow by the undying fire of His love."

Invested, among its sister communities in East and West, with the primacy conferred upon it by 'Abdu'l-Bahá's Divine Plan; armed with the mandatory provisions of His momentous Tablets; equipped with the agencies of a quarter-century-old Administrative Order, whose fabric it has reared and consolidated; encouraged by the marvelous success achieved by its daughter communities throughout the Americas, a success which has sealed the triumph of the first stage of that Plan; launched on a campaign of vaster dimensions, of superior merit, of weightier potentialities, than any it has hitherto initiated, a campaign destined to multiply its spiritual progeny in distant lands and amidst divers races, the community of the Most Great Name in the North American continent must arise, as it has never before in its history, and demonstrate anew its capacity to perform such deeds as are worthy of its high calling. Its members, the executors of 'Abdu'l-Bahá's Plan, the champion-builders of Bahá'u'lláh's embryonic Order, the torchbearers of a world-girdling civilization, must, in the years immediately ahead, bestir themselves, and, as bidden by 'Abdu'l-Bahá, "increase" their exertions "a thousandfold," lay bare further vistas in the "range" of their "future achievements" and of their "unspeakably glorious" mission, and hasten the day when, as prophesied by Him, their community will "find itself securely established upon the throne of an everlasting dominion," when "the whole earth" will be stirred and shaken by the results of its "achievements" and "resound with the praises of majesty and greatness," when America will "evolve into a center from which waves of spiritual power will emanate, and the throne of the Kingdom of God will, in the plenitude of its majesty and glory, be firmly established."

In every state of the United States, in every province of the Dominion of Canada, in every republic of Latin America, in each of the ten European countries to which its inescapable responsibilities are insistently calling it, this community, so blessed in the past, so promising at present, so dazzling in its future destiny, must, if it would guard its priceless birthright and enhance its heritage, forge ahead with equal zeal, with unrelaxing vigilance, with indomitable courage, with tireless energy, until the present stage of its mission is triumphantly concluded.

THE WORKINGS OF TWO SIMULTANEOUS PROCESSES

How could it forfeit its birthright or mar its heritage, when the country from which the vast majority of its members have sprung, the great republic of the West, government and people alike, is itself, through experiment and trial, slowly, painfully, unwittingly and irresistibly advancing towards the goal destined for it by both Bahá'u'lláh and 'Abdu'l-Bahá? Indeed if we would read aright the signs of the times, and appraise correctly the significances of contemporaneous events that are impelling forward both the American Bahá'í Community and the nation of which it forms a part on the road leading them to their ultimate destiny, we cannot fail to perceive the workings of two simultaneous processes, generated as far back as the concluding years of the Heroic Age of our Faith, each clearly defined, each distinctly separate, yet closely related and destined to culminate, in the fullness of time, in a single glorious consummation.

One of these processes is associated with the mission of the American Bahá'í Community, the other with the destiny of the American nation. The one serves directly the interests of the Administrative Order of the Faith of Bahá'u'lláh, the other promotes indirectly the institutions that are to be associated with the establishment of His World Order. The first process dates back to the revelation of those stupendous Tablets constituting the Charter of 'Abdu'l-Bahá's Divine Plan. It was held in abeyance for well-nigh twenty years while the fabric of an indispensable Administrative Order, designed as a divinely appointed agency for the operation of that Plan, was being constructed. It registered its initial success with the triumphant conclusion of the first stage of its operation in the republics of the Western Hemisphere. It signalized the opening of the second phase of its development through the inauguration of the present teaching campaign in the European continent. It must pass into the third stage of its evolution with the initiation of the third Seven Year Plan, designed to culminate in the establishment of the structure of the Administrative Order in all the remaining sovereign states and chief dependencies of the globe. It must reach the end of the first epoch in its evolution with the fulfillment of the prophecy mentioned by Daniel in the last chapter of His Book, related to the year 1335, and associated by 'Abdu'l-Bahá with the world triumph of the Faith of His Father. It will be consummated through the emergence of the Bahá'í World Commonwealth in the Golden Age of the Bahá'í Dispensation.

The other process dates back to the outbreak of the first World War that threw the great republic of the West into the vortex of the first stage of a world upheaval. It received its initial impetus through the formulation of President Wilson's Fourteen Points, closely associating for the first time that republic with the fortunes of the Old World. It suffered its first setback through the dissociation of that republic from the newly born League of Nations which that president had labored to create. It acquired added momentum through the outbreak of the second World War, inflicting unprecedented suffering on that republic, and involving it still further in the affairs of all the continents of the globe. It was further reinforced through the declaration embodied in the Atlantic Charter, as voiced by one of its chief progenitors, Franklin D. Roosevelt. It assumed a definite outline through the birth of the United Nations at the San Francisco Conference. It acquired added significance through the choice of the City of the Covenant itself as the seat of the newly born organization, through the declaration recently made by the American president related to his country's commitments in Greece and Turkey, as well as through the submission to the General Assembly of the United Nations of the thorny and challenging problem of the Holy Land, the spiritual as well as the administrative center of the World Faith of Bahá'u'lláh. It must, however long and tortuous the way, lead, through a series of victories and reverses, to the political unification of the Eastern and Western Hemispheres, to the emergence of a world government and the establishment of the Lesser Peace, as foretold by Bahá'u'lláh and foreshadowed by the Prophet Isaiah. It must, in the end, culminate in the unfurling of the banner of the Most Great Peace, in the Golden Age of the Dispensation of Bahá'u'lláh.

A Parallel Between the American Bahá'í Community and the American Republic

Might not a still closer parallel be drawn between the community singled out for the execution of this world-embracing Plan, in its relation to its sister communities, and the nation of which it forms a part, in its relation to its sister nations? On the one hand is a community which ever since its birth has been nursed in the lap of 'Abdu'l-Bahá and been lovingly trained by Him through the revelation of unnumbered Tablets, through the dispatch of special and successive messengers, and through His own prolonged visit to the North American continent in the evening of His life. It was to the members of this community, the spiritual descendants of the dawn-breakers of the Heroic Age of our Faith, that He, whilst sojourning in the City of the Covenant, chose to reveal the implications of that Covenant. It was in the vicinity of this community's earliest established center that He laid, with His own hands, the cornerstone of the first Mashriqu'l-Adhkár of the western world. It was to the members of this community that He subsequently addressed His Tablets of the Divine Plan, investing it with a spiritual primacy, and singling it out for a glorious mission among its sister communities. It was this community which won the immortal honor of being the first to introduce the Faith in the British Isles, in France and in Germany, and which sent forth its consecrated pioneers and teachers to China, Japan and India, to Australia and New Zealand, to the Balkan Peninsula, to South Africa, to Latin America, to the Baltic States, to Scandinavia and the islands of the Pacific, hoisting thereby its banner in the vast majority of the countries won over to its cause, in both the East and the West, prior to 'Abdu'l-Bahá's passing.

It was this community, the cradle and stronghold of the Administrative Order of the Faith of Bahá'u'lláh, which, on the morrow of 'Abdu'l-Bahá's ascension, was the first among all other Bahá'í communities in East and West to arise and champion the cause of that Order, to fix its pattern, to erect its fabric, to initiate its endowments, to establish and consolidate its subsidiary institutions, and to vindicate its aims and purposes. To it belongs the unique distinction of having erected, in the heart of the North American continent, the first Mashriqu'l-Adhkár of the West, the holiest edifice ever to be reared by the hands of the followers of Bahá'u'lláh in either the Eastern or Western Hemisphere. It was through the assiduous and unflagging labors of the most distinguished and consecrated among its itinerant teachers that the allegiance of royalty to the Cause of Bahá'u'lláh was won, and unequivocally proclaimed in successive testimonies as penned by the royal convert herself. To its members, the vanguard of the torchbearers of the future world civilization, must, moreover, be ascribed the imperishable glory of having launched and successfully concluded the first stage of 'Abdu'l-Bahá's Divine Plan, in the concluding years of the first Bahá'í century, establishing thereby the structural basis of the Administrative Order of the Faith in all the republics of Central and South America. It is this same community which is once again carrying off the palm of victory through launching, in the first decade of the second century of the Bahá'í Era, the second stage of that same Plan, destined to lay the foundations of the Bahá'í Administrative Order in no less than ten sovereign states in the continent of Europe, comprising the Scandinavian states, the Low Countries, the states of the Iberian Peninsula, Switzerland and Italy. And lastly, to its enterprising members must go the unique honor and privilege of having arisen, on unnumbered occasions, and over a period of more than a quarter of a century, to champion the cause of the down-trodden and persecuted among their brethren in Persia, in Egypt, in Russia, in 'Iráq and in Germany, to stretch a generous helping hand to the needy among them, to defend and safeguard the interests of their institutions, and to plead their cause before political and ecclesiastical adversaries.

On the other hand is a nation that has achieved undisputed ascendancy in the entire Western Hemisphere, whose rulers have been uniquely honored by being collectively addressed by the Author of the Bahá'í Revelation in His Kitáb-i-Aqdas; which has been acclaimed by 'Abdu'l-Bahá as the "home of the righteous and the gathering-place of the free," where the "splendors of His light shall be revealed, where the mysteries of His Faith shall be unveiled" and belonging to a continent which, as recorded by that same pen, "giveth signs and evidences of very great advancement," whose "future is even more promising," whose "influence and illumination are far-reaching," and which "will lead all nations spiritually." Moreover, it is to this great republic of the West that the Center of the Covenant of Bahá'u'lláh has referred as the nation that has "developed powers and capacities greater and more wonderful than other nations," and which "is equipped and empow-ered to accomplish that which will adorn the pages of history, to become the envy of the world, and be blest in both the East and the West for the triumph of its people." It is for this same American democracy that He expressed His fervent hope that it might be "the first nation to establish the foundation of international agreement," "to proclaim the unity of mankind," and "to unfurl the Standard of the Most Great Peace," that it might become "the distributing center of spiritual enlightenment, and all the world receive this heavenly bless-ing," and that its inhabitants might "rise from their present material attainments to such a height that heavenly illumination may stream from this center to all the peoples of the world." It is in connection with its people that He has affirmed that they are "indeed worthy of being the first to build the Tabernacle of the Great Peace and proclaim the oneness of mankind."

THE UNITED STATES IS SIGNALLY BLEST

This nation so signally blest, occupying so eminent and responsible a position in a continent so wonderfully endowed, was the first among the nations of the West to be warmed and illuminated by the rays of the Revelation of Bahá'u'lláh, soon after the proclamation of His Covenant on the morrow of His ascension. This nation, moreover, may well claim to have, as a result of its effective participation in both the first and second world wars, redressed the balance, saved mankind the horrors of devastation and bloodshed involved in the prolongation of hostilities, and decisively contributed, in the course of the latter conflict, to the overthrow of the exponents of ideologies fundamentally at variance with the universal tenets of our Faith.

To her President, the immortal Woodrow Wilson, must be ascribed the unique honor, among the statesmen of any nation, whether of the East or of the West, of having voiced sentiments so akin to the principles animating the Cause of Bahá'u'lláh, and of having more than any other world leader, contributed to the creation of the League of Nations—achievements which the pen of the Center of God's Covenant acclaimed as signalizing the dawn of the Most Great Peace, whose sun, according to that same pen, must needs arise as the direct consequence of the enforcement of the laws of the Dispensation of Bahá'u'lláh.

To the matchless position achieved by so preeminent a president of the American Union, in a former period, at so critical a juncture in international affairs, must now be added the splendid initiative taken, in recent years by the American government, culminating in the birth of the successor of that League in San Francisco, and the establishment of its permanent seat in the city of New York. Nor can the preponderating influence exerted by this nation in the councils of the world, the prodigious economic and political power that it wields, the prestige it enjoys, the wealth of which it disposes, the idealism that animates its people, her magnificent contribution, as a result of her unparalleled productive power, for the relief of human suffering and the rehabilitation of peoples and nations, be overlooked in a survey of the position which she holds, and which distinguishes her from her sister nations in both the new and old worlds.

Tribulations Are Inevitable

Many and divers are the setbacks and reverses which this nation, extolled so highly by 'Abdu'l-Bahá, and occupying at present so unique a position among its fellow nations, must, alas, suffer. The road leading to its destiny is long, thorny and tortuous. The impact of various forces upon the structure and polity of that nation will be tremendous. Tribulations, on a scale unprecedented in its history, and calculated to purge its institutions, to purify the hearts of its people, to fuse its constituent elements, and to weld it into one entity with its sister nations in both hemispheres, are inevitable.

In one of the most remarkable Tablets revealed by 'Abdu'l-Bahá, passages of which have already been quoted on previous occasions, written in the evening of His life, soon after the termination of the first World War, He anticipates, in succinct and ominous sentences, the successive ebullitions which must afflict humanity, and whose full force the American nation must, if her destiny is to be accomplished, inevitably experience. "The ills from which the world now suffers," He wrote, "will multiply; the gloom which envelops it will deepen. The Balkans will remain discontented. Its restlessness will increase. The vanquished powers will continue to agitate. They will resort to every measure that may rekindle the flame of war. Movements, newly born and world-wide in their range, will exert their utmost effort for the advancement of their designs. The Movement of the Left will acquire great importance. Its influence will spread."

The agitation in the Balkan Peninsula; the feverish activity in which Germany and Italy played a disastrous role, culminating in the outbreak of the second World War; the rise of the Fascist and Nazi movements, which spread their ramifications to distant parts of the globe; the spread of communism which, as a result of the victory of Soviet Russia in that same war, has been greatly accelerated—all these happenings, some unequivocally, others in veiled language, have been forecast in this Tablet, the full force of whose implications are as yet undisclosed, and which, we may well anticipate, the American nation, as yet insufficiently schooled by adversity, must sooner or later experience.

AMERICA TO EVOLVE UNTIL LAST TASK IS DISCHARGED

Whatever the Hand of a beneficent and inscrutable Destiny has reserved for this youthful, this virile, this idealistic, this spiritually blessed and enviable nation, however severe the storms which may buffet it in the days to come in either hemisphere, however sweeping the changes which the impact of cataclysmic forces from without, and the stirrings of a Divine embryonic Order from within, will effect in its structure and life, we may, confident in the words uttered by 'Abdu'l-Bahá, feel assured that that great republic—the shell that enshrines so precious a member of the world community of the followers of His Father—will continue to evolve, undivided and undefeatable, until the sum total of its contributions to the birth, the rise and the fruition of that world civilization, the child of the Most Great Peace and hallmark of the Golden Age of the Dispensation of Bahá'u'lláh, will have been made, and its last task discharged.

[June 5, 1947]

European Pioneers and Temple Contract

Rejoice at evidences of continued vigorous activity. Renew plea to believers possessing independent means to volunteer for European pioneer field, both settlers and itinerant teachers. Eagerly awaiting response to Convention message. Praying for placing of Temple contract before termination of current year. Ardently supplicating unprecedented blessings for manifold, meritorious, magnificent services. Deepest love.

[July 13, 1947]

Evidences of Notable Expansion

Greatly welcome evidences of a notable expansion of activities and increased intensification of efforts for publicity. I urge believers and local assemblies to redouble their efforts in support of vital National Fund. Praying ardently for realization of your highest hopes. Appreciate action for preservation of Keith's grave. Do not advise you to transmit further funds to Persia for the grave. I appeal to North American believers to exert their utmost to insure the formation of required number of assemblies by next April. Further sacrifices demanded, rich reward assured. May entire body of American believers arise to fulfill their glorious destiny.

Abiding gratitude, deepest love.

[September 10, 1947]

Effective Prosecution of Sacred Tasks

The steadily deepening crisis which mankind is traversing, on the morrow of the severest ordeal it has yet suffered, and the attendant tribulations and commotions which a travailing age must necessarily experience, as a prelude to the birth of the new World Order, destined to rise upon the ruins of a tottering civilization, must, as they intensify, increasingly influence the course, and, in some cases, retard the progress, of the collective enterprises successively launched in the opening years of the second Bahá'í century, and in almost every continent of the globe, by the world-wide community of the organized followers of the Faith of Bahá'u'lláh. In the land of its birth long-standing political rivalries, combined with a steady decline in the authority and influence exercised by the central government, are contributing to the reemergence of reactionary forces, represented by an as yet influential and fanatical priesthood, to a recrudescence of the persecution, and a multiplication of the disabilities, to which a still unemancipated Faith has been so cruelly subjected for more than a century. In the heart of the continent of Europe, still fiercer political rivalries, as well as the clash of conflicting ideologies, have prevented the unification, indefinitely retarded the national revival, multiplied the vicissitudes and rendered more desperate the plight, of a nation comprising within its frontiers the largest community of the adherents of the Faith on that continent—a community destined, as prophesied by 'Abdu'l-Bahá, to play a major role in the spiritual awakening and the ultimate conversion of the European peoples and races to His Father's Faith. In the subcontinent of India recent political developments of a momentous character have plunged its divers castes, races and denominations into grave turmoil, brought in their wake riots, bloodshed, misery and confusion, fanned into flame religious animosities, and well-nigh disrupted its economic life. In the Nile Valley the outbreak of a widespread and virulent epidemic, following closely upon the political unrest and the severe economic crisis already afflicting its inhabitants, threatens to disorganize the life of the nation and to bring in its wake afflictions of an even more serious character. In the Holy Land itself, the heart and nerve-center of the far-flung and firmly knit community of the followers of Bahá'u'lláh, and the repository of its holiest shrines, already gravely disturbed by the chronic instability of its political life, the religious dissensions of its inhabitants, and the ten-year-long strain and danger to which its people have been subjected and exposed, fresh perils are looming on its horizon, menacing it, on the one hand with the ravages of an epidemic that has already taken so heavy a toll of the lives of the people beyond its southern frontier, and threatening it, on the other, with a civil war of extreme severity and unpredictable in its consequences. Subject to the same fundamental causes which have deranged the equilibrium of present-day society and corroded its life are to be regarded the privations, the restrictions and crisis which, to a lesser degree, are oppressing the peoples of Central and Southeastern Europe, of the British Isles and of certain republics of Central and South America.

In all these territories, whether in the Eastern or Western Hemisphere, the nascent institutions of a struggling Faith, though subjected in varying degrees to the stress and strain associated with the decline and dissolution of time-honored institutions, with fratricidal strife, economic upheavals, financial crises, outbreaks of epidemics and political revolutions, have thus far, through the interpositions of a merciful Providence, been graciously enabled to follow their charted course, undeflected by the cross-currents and the tempestuous winds which must of necessity increasingly agitate human society ere the hour of its ultimate redemption approaches.

In contrast to these sorely tried countries on the European, the Asiatic and the African continents, unlike her sister republics in either Central or South America, the great republic of the West—the homeland of that mother community which, fostered through the tender care of an ever-solicitous Master, has already proved itself capable of rearing in its turn such splendid progeny among the divers communities of Latin America, which bids fair to multiply its daughter communities in a continent of mightier potentialities—such a republic has been, to a peculiar degree and over a long and uninterrupted period, relatively free from the chronic disorders, the political disturbances, the economic convulsions, the communal riots, the epidemics, the religious persecutions, the privations and loss of life which, during successive generations, have in one way or another afflicted so many peoples in almost every part of the globe.

Singled out by the Almighty for such a unique measure of favor, suffered to evolve, untrammelled and unperturbed, within the shell of its God-given Administrative Order, distinguished from its sister communities through the revelation of a Plan emanating directly from the mind and pen of its Founder, enriched already by so many trophies, each an eloquent testimony to its missionary zeal and valor in distant fields and amidst divers peoples, the Community of the Most Great Name in the North American continent must, sensible of the abounding grace vouchsafed to it by Bahá'u'lláh, resolve, as it has never resolved before, to carry out, however much it may be buffeted by future circumstances and the unforeseen ordeals which a heedless and chaotic world may still further experience, the mission confidently entrusted to its hands by an all-wise and loving Master.

HEART-WARMING PROGRESS IN EUROPEAN ENTERPRISE

Already in the newly opened European field, where the first stage of its transatlantic missionary enterprise is now unfolding, the success which the vanguard of its army of pioneers has already achieved in several leading capitals of that continent is truly heart-warming and evokes intense admiration. The broad outlines of the primary institutions heralding the erection of the administrative framework of the Faith of Bahá'u'lláh in no less than ten sovereign states of Europe can already be discerned—a powerful and signal reinforcement of the organized and progressive efforts exerted by the British and German communities on the northwestern limits of that continent and in its very heart. In the Latin American field, where the structural basis of a rising Administrative Order has already been established, through the formation of firmly grounded assemblies in each of the republics of Central and South America, the stage is being set for the erection of those institutions which are to be regarded as the harbingers of the secondary Houses of Justice which, in each of these republics, must act as pillars, and assist in sustaining the weight, of the final unit designed to consummate the institutions of that order. On the northern portion of that same hemisphere the stage is already set for the impending emergence of an institution which, however circumscribed its basis, must ultimately, directly participate in the measures preliminary to the constitution of the Universal House of Justice.

A community now in the process of marshalling and directing, in such vast territories, in such outlying regions, amidst such a diversity of peoples, at so precarious a stage in the fortunes of mankind, forces of such incalculable potency, to serve purposes so meritorious and lofty, cannot afford to falter for a moment or retrace its steps on the path it now travels. Its commitments, so vast, so challenging, so rich in their potentialities, in the North American continent, must, whatever betide it, be carried out, in their entirety and without the slightest reservation or hesitation. The pledge to multiply the local administrative institutions, throughout the length and breadth of this continent must be honored, and the placing of the contract for the interior ornamentation of the holiest House of Worship ever to be erected to the glory of Bahá'u'lláh expedited. Above all a prodigious effort, nationwide, sustained and wholly unprecedented in the annals of a richly endowed and spiritually blessed community, aiming at the immediate increase of the financial resources required for the effective prosecution of its manifold and pressing tasks, is required.

TRIPLE CAMPAIGN OF CRITICAL IMPORTANCE

The triple campaign, conducted in two hemispheres, comprising within the scope of its operation the entire territory of the North American republic, the Dominion of Canada, twenty republics of Latin America, and no less than ten sovereign states of the European continent, is indeed of critical importance. Every phase of this threefold crusade, undertaken at the dawn of the second Bahá'í century by the executors of 'Abdu'l-Bahá's Will and the custodians of His Plan, must be accorded its due measure of consideration and its needs simultaneously and vigorously fulfilled. The allurements of the glorious adventure in the Latin American field; the glittering prizes already won and the new ones within reach, must, at no time, obscure the issues, or retard the task confronting the prosecutors of the Plan in their homeland, or allow the interests of its assemblies, for the most part new and struggling, to be either neglected or forgotten. Nor must the glamor of the still more recent and glorious adventure embarked upon across the Atlantic, within a turbulent, politically convulsed, economically disrupted and spiritually depleted continent, dim, in however small a measure, the radiance, or detract from the urgency, of the magnificent enterprises, whose first fruits in Latin America are only beginning to mature, in direct consequence of the initial operation of the Plan bequeathed by 'Abdu'l-Bahá to the American believers.

To the vital requirements of this Plan, at so critical a juncture, both in the fortunes of mankind in general, and of the Plan itself, to which detailed reference has been made in a previous communication, I need not again refer. All I desire to emphasize is my fervent plea, addressed to both the administrators who, as the elected representatives of the community must devise the plans, coordinate the activities, and direct the agencies of a continually expanding community, and to those whose privilege it is to labor, at home and abroad, to insure the effective prosecution of these sacred tasks, to realize the propitiousness of the present hour, recognize its urgency, meet its challenge and appreciate its unique potentialities. As the international situation worsens, as the fortunes of mankind sink to a still lower ebb, the momentum of the Plan must be further accelerated, and the concerted exertions of the community responsible for its execution rise to still higher levels of consecration and heroism. As the fabric of present-day society heaves and cracks under the strain and stress of portentous events and calamities, as the fissures, accentuating the cleavage separating nation from nation, class from class, race from race, and creed from creed, multiply, the prosecutors of the Plan must evince a still greater cohesion in their spiritual lives and administrative activities, and demonstrate a higher standard of concerted effort, of mutual assistance, and of harmonious development in their collective enterprises.

Then, and only then, will the reaction to the stupendous forces, released through the operation of a divinely conceived, divinely impelled Plan, be made apparent, and the fairest fruit of the weightiest spiritual enterprise launched in recorded history under the aegis of the Center of the Covenant of Bahá'u'lláh be garnered.

[October 25, 1947]

Recognition of Preeminent Services

Highly gratified at unceasing, compelling evidences of exalted spirit of Bahá'í stewardship animating American Bahá'í Community, as attested by the alacrity of its national representatives in executing the first Temple contract, their promptitude in extending effective assistance to their Persian brethren, their vigilance in safeguarding integrity of the Faith in the City of the Covenant and their vigor in prosecuting the national campaign of publicity.

In recognition of preeminent services continually enriching the record of achievements associated with preeminent community of the Bahá'í world, I am arranging transfer of extensive, valuable property acquired in precincts of Shrines on Mount Carmel to name of Palestine Branch of American Assembly.

Happy to announce completion of plans and specifications for erection of arcade surrounding the Báb's Sepulcher, constituting the first step in the process destined to culminate in construction of the dome anticipated by 'Abdu'l-Bahá and marking consummation of enterprise initiated by Him fifty years ago according to instructions given Him by Bahá'u'lláh.

[December 15, 1947]

Critical Stage of Task on Home Front

I am deeply concerned at critical stage of task confronting North American Teaching Committee, constituting at this juncture the paramount objective of present Plan. Owing to urgent, overriding importance of Committee's responsibility and to swiftly approaching time limit fixed for attainment of the goal of one hundred seventy-five assemblies, emergency measures carefully, promptly devised by national representatives of the community and wholeheartedly supported by entire mass of the believers of the North American continent, designed to safeguard the existing assemblies and rapidly multiply their number, are imperative. The placing of further contract for Temple, the reinforcement of basis of forthcoming Canadian National Spiritual Assembly, the additional consolidation of the institutions of the Faith in Latin America, the wider proclamation of its message to the masses, even the multiplication of pioneers in the European field, should be unhesitatingly subordinated to demands of the one disconcerting aspect of an otherwise successfully conducted Plan. I address this last-minute appeal to every single member of the community, the champion warriors in the army of Bahá'u'lláh, which since launching the Plan formulated by the Center of His Covenant never succumbed to defeat nor was thwarted in its purpose, to arise resolutely, volunteer instantly to fill the gap in the main defenses of the home front and register total victory ere the termination of the second year of the Second Seven Year Plan. Fervently praying for instantaneous, decisive response.

[January 10, 1948]

No Sacrifice Too Great

The gravity of the emergency facing the North American believers is unprecedented since the initiation of the Divine Plan and unparalleled in the history of the American Bahá'í Community since 'Abdu'l-Bahá's passing. No obstacle is insuperable, no sacrifice too great for attainment of supremely important objective. The eyes of her sister communities in every continent of the globe and of her daughter communities of Latin America, handicapped by a variety of adverse circumstances, are fixed upon the community of followers of Bahá'u'lláh in North American continent who are enjoying the blessings of internal peace, adequate resources, administrative experience and organizing ability for their divinely appointed mission, expecting them to arise and avert the reverse which would mar the splendor of their record of unexampled stewardship. I am moved to plead, at this eleventh hour, that the rank and file of the community, particularly the members resident in long-established leading strongholds of the Faith—New York, Chicago, Los Angeles, San Francisco, Washington —issue forth unhesitatingly, determinedly, sacrifice every interest, assume positions in the forefront of the struggle and emulate in the course of the first decade of second Bahá'í century, opening years of the second epoch of Formative Age of the Faith, exploits of their spiritual progenitors, the dawn-breakers of the Heroic Age, which immortalized the dawn of the first Bahá'í century. The immediate fortunes of the Plan are precariously hanging in the balance. The three months' interval is swiftly running out. My heart aches at contemplation of the possibility of failure of the stalwart community to rise to the heights of the occasion. I refuse to believe that its members, invested with unique apostolic mission of 'Abdu'l-Bahá, will shrink from meeting the most challenging requirement of the present hour.

[February 1, 1948]

Prevailing Crisis

Hope is welling up in my anxious, overburdened heart that the North American Bahá'í Community may yet emerge triumphant over the prevailing crisis, demonstrate its capacity to preserve its hard-won prizes and redeem its pledges through a further display of its qualities of unconquerable faith, unbreakable solidarity, dauntless valor and heroic self-sacrifice, and vindicate its right to primacy in the world community of the followers of Bahá'u'lláh. High water mark is still unattained notwithstanding the mounting tide of enthusiastic response displayed by an aroused community. Dangerous passage now forded in this eleventh-hour campaign. I am fervently praying that further intensification of effort, sustained, coordinated, consecrated and unanimously exerted, will sweep its members on crest of the wave to total victory. I feel assured that cumulative efforts of participants in emergency campaign launched by entire community will increasingly attract the promised inflowing grace of the holy Author of its destinies, will demonstrate afresh its worthiness of the paternal care of its divine Founder, will win added commendation from its sister communities of the Eastern Hemisphere, deepen the admiration and inspire the emulation of its daughter communities in Latin America and the European continent, and strengthen the attachment and reinforce the brotherly affection of its Guardian.

[February 13, 1948]

Emergency Teaching Campaign

Greatly encouraged by the splendid progress of the tremendous drive initiated in response to my appeal. The zero hour is inexorably approaching. Nineteen additional settlers can and must be provided. Praying with increasing fervor for total success, complete victory.

[April 6, 1948]

Marvelous Acceleration

[FIRST MESSAGE TO 1948 CONVENTION]

I am moved to share with assembled delegates of the fortieth American Bahá'í Convention the following facts and figures testifying to the present status of the World Faith of Bahá'u'lláh and disclosing the marvelous acceleration in the double process of the extension of its range and the consolidation of the institutions of its Administrative Order in the Eastern and Western Hemispheres in the course of the first four years of the second Bahá'í century.

The number of countries opened to the Faith total ninety-one. Bahá'í literature is translated and printed in fifty-one languages. Representatives of thirty-one races are enrolled in the Bahá'í World Community. Eighty-eight assemblies, national and local, are incorporated. The number of localities where Bahá'ís have established residence has been raised to over thirty in Australasia, to over forty in Germany and Austria, over sixty in the Dominion of Canada, over eighty in the Indian subcontinent and Burma, over one hundred in Latin America, over seven hundred in Persia and to over twelve hundred in the United States of America.

The value of international Bahá'í endowments in the Holy Land and the Jordan Valley is estimated at over six hundred thousand pounds. National Bahá'í endowments on the North American continent are valued at over two million dollars. The area of land dedicated to the Mashriqu'l-Adhkár in Persia is approximately four million square meters. The value of the national Hazíratu'l-Quds in the capitals of India and Persia respectively is six hundred thousand rupees and fifty thousand pounds. The area of land dedicated to the first Mashriqu'l-Adhkár in South America is ninety thousand square meters. The number of pieces of Bahá'í literature sold and distributed in the course of one year in North America is over eighty thousand pieces. The record of the number of visitors to the Mashriqu'l-Adhkár in America in one year is over seventeen thousand and the total number of visitors since its erection is over one quarter of a million. The number of states in the American Union formally recognizing Bahá'í marriage certificates is now eight. The number of national assemblies functioning in the Bahá'í world is raised to nine through the formation of the first Canadian National Assembly, to be shortly reinforced through the constitution of two additional assemblies in South and Central America and the West Indies.

The second seven-year, the six-year, the four and one-half year, the six-year, the three-year, the five-year and forty-five month plans, respectively launched by the American, British, Indian, Australasian, 'Iráqí, Canadian, and Persian National Spiritual Assemblies, some culminating at the first Centennial of the birth of Bahá'u'lláh's mission, others the Hundredth Anniversary of the Báb's Martyrdom, are aiming at the establishment of three national assemblies in Canada and Latin America, the completion of the interior ornamentation of the Mother Temple of the West, the formation of spiritual assemblies in ten sovereign states of the European continent, the constitution of nineteen assemblies in the British Isles, doubling the number of assemblies in India, Pakistan and Burma, the reconstitution of the dissolved assemblies and the establishment of ninety-five new centers in Persia, the conversion of groups in Bahrein, the Ḥijáz and Afghánistán into assemblies, the formation of administrative nuclei in the Arabian territories of Yemen, Oman, Hasa and Kuweit; the formation of thirty-one groups and seven assemblies in Australia, New Zealand and Tasmania; the multiplication of centers in the provinces of 'Iráq, including the district of Shaṭṭu'l-Arab; the incorporation of the Canadian National Assembly; doubling the number of assemblies and raising to one hundred the centers in the Dominion of Canada; the constitution of nuclei in Newfoundland and Greenland and the participation of Eskimos and Red Indians in the local institutions of the Administrative Order.

Plans and specifications have been prepared, and preliminary measures taken, to place contracts for the arcade of the Báb's Sepulcher. Historic International Bahá'í Congresses held in South and Central America and an inter-European Teaching Conference projected for Geneva paving the way for future World Bahá'í Congress. Recognition extended to the Faith by United Nations as international non-governmental body, enabling appointment of accredited representatives to United Nations conferences, is heralding world recognition for a universal proclamation of the Faith of Bahá'u'lláh.

[April 16, 1948]

Brilliant Achievements

[SECOND MESSAGE TO 1948 CONVENTION]

Joyfully acclaim brilliant achievements transcending fondest hopes and setting the seal of complete victory on the stupendous labors undertaken by American Bahá'í Community in the second year of the Second Seven Year Plan. The constitution of the National Spiritual

Assembly of Canada, the heroic feat of raising to almost two hundred the number of spiritual assemblies in the North American continent, the marvelous expansion of the daughter communities in Latin America, the successful conclusion of the preliminary phase of the interior ornamentation of the Mashriqu'l-Adhkár, and the crowning exploit of the formation of no less than seven assemblies in the newly opened transcontinental field, endow with everlasting fame the second epoch of the Formative Age, immeasurably enrich the annals of the opening decade of the second Bahá'í century, and constitute a landmark in the unfoldment of the second stage of the execution of 'Abdu'l-Bahá's Plan.

The primacy of the American Bahá'í Community is reasserted, fully vindicated and completely safeguarded. Recent successive victories proclaim the undiminished strength and exemplary valor of the rank and file of the community whether administrators, teachers or pioneers in three continents regarded as the latest links in the chain of uninterrupted achievements performed by its members in the council, and teaching field for over a quarter of a century. I recall on this joyous occasion with pride, emotion, thankfulness, the resplendent record of stewardship of this dearly loved, richly endowed, unflinchingly resolute community, whose administrators have assumed the preponderating share in perfecting the machinery of the Administrative Order, whose elected representatives have raised the edifice and completed the exterior ornamentation of the Mother Temple of the West, whose trailblazers opened an overwhelming majority of the ninety-one countries now included within the pale of the Faith, whose pioneers established flourishing communities in twenty republics of Latin America, whose benefactors extended in ample measure assistance in various ways to their sorely pressed brethren in distant fields, whose members scattered themselves to thirteen hundred centers in every state of the American Union, every province of the Dominion of Canada, whose firmest champion succeeded in winning royalty's allegiance to the Message of Bahá'u'lláh, whose heroes and martyrs laid down their lives in its service in fields as remote as Honolulu, Buenos Aires, Sidney, Iṣfáhán, whose vanguard pushed its outposts to the antipodes on the farthest verge of the South American continent, to the vicinity of the Arctic Circle, to the northern, southern, and western fringes of the European continent, whose ambassadors are now convening, on the soil of one of the newly won territories, its historic first conference designed to consolidate the newly won prizes, whose spokesmen are securing recognition of the institutions of Bahá'u'lláh's rising World Order in the United Nations.

Appeal to members of the community so privileged, so loved, so valorous, endowed with such potentialities to unitedly press forward however afflictive the trials their countrymen may yet experience, however grievous the tribulations the land of their heart's desire may yet suffer, however oppressive an anxiety the temporary severance of external communications with the World Center of their Faith may engender, however onerous the tasks still to be accomplished, until every single obligation under the present Plan is honorably fulfilled, enabling them to launch in its appointed time the third crusade destined to bring glorious consummation to the first epoch in the evolution of their divinely appointed world mission, fulfill the prophecy uttered by Daniel over twenty centuries ago, contribute the major share of the world triumph of the Faith of Bahá'u'lláh envisaged by the Center of His Covenant, and hasten the opening of the Golden Age of the Bahá'í Dispensation.

[April 26, 1948]

Support the National Fund

Temple drawings received. Approve design. Urge that you proceed without delay to place Temple contracts.

I appeal to entire body of believers to arise and generously support the National Fund in hour of greatest need to insure uninterrupted progress in the ornamentation of the House of Worship which, as foretold by 'Abdu'l-Bahá, is already conferring such benefits upon the community.

[May 4, 1948]

Temple Interior Ornamentation and Arcade of the Báb's Sepulcher

Delighted at contract for ornamentation, projected reception (i.e., for UN delegates in Geneva), appointment of new committees for consolidation of teaching work and noble determination to pursue unremittingly your God-given task.

Announce to the friends that signature on contracts for arcade of the Báb's Sepulcher is synchronizing with first contract for interior ornamentation of the Mother Temple of the West.

[May 14, 1948]

My Appeal to This God-Chosen Community

The response of the American Bahá'í Community to the urgent call to arise and remedy a critical situation has been such as to excite my highest admiration and exceed the hopes of all those who had waited with anxious hearts for this dangerous corner to be turned at such an important stage in the prosecution of the Second Seven Year Plan.

The rapidity with which the challenge has been met, the strenuous efforts which have been systematically exerted, the zeal and devotion which have been so abundantly demonstrated, the resolution and self-sacrifice which have been so strikingly displayed by the members of a community, burdened with such mighty responsibilities and intent on maintaining its lead among its sister communities in East and West, confer great luster on this latest episode in the history of the prosecution of the Divine Plan. I am moved to offer its high-minded and valiant members my heartfelt congratulations on so conspicuous a victory, and on the preservation of an unblemished record of achievements in the service of the Faith of Bahá'u'lláh.

The formation of the Canadian National Assembly, the conclusion of the preliminary steps for the completion of the interior ornamentation of the Mashriqu'l-Adhkár, the rapid multiplication and consolidation of the institutions of the Faith throughout Latin America, the steady expansion of the activities aiming at the proclamation of the Faith to the masses, the recognition secured, on behalf of the national institutions of a world community, from the United Nations Organization, above all the phenomenal success achieved through the constitution of no less than eight spiritual assemblies in seven of the goal countries selected as targets for the transatlantic operation of the Plan, now crowned by the holding of the first teaching conference on the continent of Europe—all these have served to immortalize the second year of the Second Seven Year Plan and round out the mighty feat accomplished throughout the states and provinces of the North American continent—the base from which the operation of a divinely impelled and constantly expanding Plan are being conducted.

Emboldened by the enduring and momentous successes won, on so many fronts, in such distant fields, among such a diversity of peoples, and in the face of such formidable obstacles, by a community now launched, in both hemispheres, on its world-encircling mission, I direct my appeal to the entire membership of this God-chosen community, to its associates and daughter communities in the Dominion of Canada, in Central and South America, and in the continent of Europe, to proclaim, in the course of this current year, to their sister communities in East and West and by deeds no less resplendent than those of the past, their inflexible resolve to prosecute unremittingly the Plan entrusted to their care, and emblazon on their shields the emblems of new victories in its service.

The placing, with care and promptitude, of the successive contracts, designed to ensure the uninterrupted progress of the interior ornamentation of the Temple, at a time when the international situation is fraught with so many complications and perils; the acceleration of the twofold process designed to preserve the status of the present assemblies throughout the states of the Union and multiply their number; the constant broadening of the bases on which the projected Latin American national assemblies are to be securely founded; the steady expansion of the work initiated to give wider publicity to the Faith in the North American continent and in circles associated with the United Nations; and, last but not least, the constitution of firmly established assemblies in each of the remaining goal countries in Europe and the simultaneous initiation, in the countries already provided with such assemblies, of measures aiming at the formation of several nuclei calculated to reinforce the structural basis of an infant Administrative Order—these stand out as the primary and inescapable duties which the members of your Assembly—the mainspring of the multitudinous activities carried on in your homeland, in the Latin American field, and on the European front—must in this third year of the Second Seven Year Plan, befittingly discharge.

That the launching of one of these fundamental activities to be

conducted by your Assembly during the present year—the commencement of the interior ornamentation of the Mother Temple of the
West—should have so closely synchronized with the placing of the first
two contracts for the completion of the Sepulcher of the Báb, as
contemplated by 'Abdu'l-Bahá, is indeed a phenomenon of singular
significance. This conjunction of two events of historic importance,
linking, in a peculiar degree, the most sacred House of Worship in the
American continent with the most hallowed Shrine on the slopes of
Mount Carmel, brings vividly to mind the no less remarkable coinci-
dence marking the simultaneous holding, on a Naw-Rúz Day, of the
first convention of the American Bahá'í Community and the entombment by the Center of Bahá'u'lláh's Covenant of the remains of the Báb
in the newly constructed vault of His Shrine.[1] The simultaneous arrival
of those remains in the fortress city of 'Akká and of the first pilgrims
from the continent of America;[2] the subsequent association of the
founder of the American Bahá'í Community with 'Abdu'l-Bahá in the
laying of the cornerstone of the Báb's Mausoleum on Mount Carmel;
the holding of the Centenary of His Declaration beneath the dome of
the recently constructed Mashriqu'l-Adhkár at Wilmette, on which
solemn occasion His blessed portrait was unveiled, on western soil, to
the eyes of His followers; and the unique distinction now conferred on
a member[3] of the North American Bahá'í Community of designing the
dome, envisaged by 'Abdu'l-Bahá, as the final and essential embellishment of the Bab's Sepulcher—all these have served to associate the
Herald of our Faith and His resting-place with the fortunes of a
community which has so nobly responded to His summons addressed to
the "peoples of the West" in His Qayyúmu'l-Asmá'.

"This Sublime Shrine has remained unbuilt . . . ," 'Abdu'l-Bahá,
looking at the Shrine from the steps of His House on an August day in
1915, remarked to some of His companions, at a time when the Báb's
remains had already been placed by Him in the vault of one of the six
chambers He had already constructed for that purpose. "God willing, it
will be accomplished. We have carried its construction to this stage."

The initiation in these days of extreme peril in the Holy Land of so
great and holy an enterprise, founded by Bahá'u'lláh Himself whilst
still a Prisoner in 'Akká and commenced by 'Abdu'l-Bahá during the
darkest and most perilous days of His ministry, recalls to our minds,

furthermore, the construction of the superstructure of the Temple in
Wilmette during one of the severest financial crises that has afflicted
the United States of America, and the completion of its exterior
ornamentation during the dark days of the last World War. Indeed, the
tragic and moving story of the transfer of the Báb's mutilated body from
place to place ever since His Martyrdom in Tabríz, its fifty-year
concealment in Persia; its perilous and secret journey by way of Ṭihrán,
Isfáhán, Kirmánshán, Baghdád, Damascus, Beirut and 'Akká to the
Mountain of God, its ultimate resting place; its concealment for a further period of ten years in the Holy Land itself; the vexatious and long-
drawn-out negotiations for the purchase of the site chosen by
Bahá'u'lláh Himself for its entombment; the threats of 'Abdu'l-Ḥamíd,
the Turkish tyrant, the accusations levelled against its Trustee, the
plots devised, and the inspection made, by the scheming members of
the notorious Turkish Commission of Inquiry; the perils to which the
bloodthirsty Jamál Páshá exposed it; the machinations of the archbreaker of Bahá'u'lláh's Covenant, of His brother and of His son,
respectively, aiming at the frustration of 'Abdu'l-Bahá's design, at the
prevention of the sale of land within the precincts of the Shrine itself,
and the multiplication of the measures taken for the preservation and
consolidation of the properties purchased in its vicinity and dedicated
to it—all these are to be regarded as successive stages in the history of
the almost hundred year long process destined to culminate in the
consummation of Bahá'u'lláh's irresistible purpose of erecting a lasting
and befitting memorial to His Divine Herald and Co-Founder of His
Faith.

As the mission entrusted by 'Abdu'l-Bahá to the followers of His
Faith in the North American continent gathers momentum, unfolds its
potentialities, and raises to new heights of heroism and renown its
valiant prosecutors, events of still greater significance will, no doubt,
transpire, which will serve to enhance the value of the work which the
prosecutors of the Plan are carrying out, to widen their vision, to
reinforce their exertions, to sustain their spirit, to ennoble their heritage, to noise abroad their fame, to facilitate their assumption of the
unique functions distinguishing their stewardship to the Faith, and to
hasten the advent of the day, which shall witness, in the Golden Age
that is still unborn, their "elevation to the throne of an everlasting

dominion," the day whereon "the whole earth" will "resound with the praises" of their "majesty and greatness."

[May 18, 1948]
 ¹ See *God Passes By*, p. 276
 ² See *God Passes By*, p. 257-8
 ³ William Sutherland Maxwell of Montreal

Urge Special Attention to Goals

Welcome decisions made at recent Assembly meeting. Supplicating blessings for forthcoming conference with committees. Elated by magnificent success achieved at European Conference, development of affiliation with United Nations . . . Urge you devote special attention in current year to insure rapid progress of Temple construction, maintenance of assembly status and consolidation of newly, formed assemblies.

[June 23, 1948]

Praying for Added Fervor

Greatly welcome initiated plans for schools, delighted at progress of Temple work, acceptance of resolutions by UNO Conference, election of Ioas. Urge unrelaxing vigilance in maintenance of status and consolidation of assemblies in North America, to insure steady expansion of manifold activities in Latin America and Europe. Praying for added fervor, speedy realization of high objectives of God-given mission of much-admired American Bahá'í Community.

[August 9, 1948]

Completed Tasks Release Outpouring of Grace

Welcome Assembly's high resolve to insure uninterrupted Temple construction. Deeply moved and thankful for continued evidence of the inflexible determination with which the rank and file of the clear-sighted, high-minded, divinely sustained American Bahá'í Community, its representatives, national, local and regional, its pioneers at home and overseas, discharge in distant fields, despite the smallness of their numbers and their limited resources, tasks of such vast dimensions, of so diversified a character, of such great moment, at so significant a stage in the declining fortunes of an imperiled society. I feel convinced that unflinching maintenance of so exalted a standard of stewardship at the threshold of Bahá'u'lláh must release in still greater measure the outpouring of His grace so essential and befitting the consummation of a Divine Plan deriving its authority from the pen of the Center of His Covenant and propelled by agencies created through the generative influence of His Will and Testament.

[September 14, 1948]

Appeal to Entire Community to Persevere

Appreciate Assembly's message. Praying for success of plans. Urge special effort to expedite work of Temple, reinforce pioneer endeavor in Europe owing to deteriorating international situation. Appeal to entire community wholeheartedly to persevere irrespective of darkened outlook.

[October 21, 1948]

Scale Nobler Heights of Heroism

The deepening crisis ominously threatening further to derange the equilibrium of a politically convulsed, economically disrupted, socially subverted, morally decadent and spiritually moribund society is testing the tenacity, taxing the resources and challenging the spirit throughout three continents of the chosen trustees and valiant executors of 'Abdu'l-Bahá's Divine Plan. This present hour, however critical, fraught with uncertainty, cannot and must not retard the unfoldment of the manifold tasks so brilliantly inaugurated, so diligently prosecuted, so dazzling in their prospects.

The record of the Bahá'í community since inception of the Formative Age conclusively demonstrates that accomplishment of signal acts accompanied, or followed upon, periods of acute distress in European and American contemporary history. The machinery of the Administrative Order was established, and preliminary stage of construction of the House of Worship was undertaken, by a grief-stricken community in the anxious years following the sudden removal of its loving, watchful Founder. The superstructure of the Temple was erected amid the strain and stress of an economic depression of an unprecedented severity gripping the North American continent. The first Seven Year Plan, opening stage in the execution of the historic mission entrusted to the American Bahá'í Community, was launched in the face of a gathering storm culminating in the direst conflict yet experienced by mankind. The Tablets of the Divine Plan were revealed amidst the turmoil of the first World War involving great danger to the life of their Author. The remains of 'Abdu'l-Bahá's mother and brother were transferred to site of monuments constituting focus of institutions of future World Administrative Center and erected on the morrow of the outbreak of hostilities while the Holy Land was increasingly exposed to the perils precipitated by the second conflict. The daughter communities of Latin America were called into being and exterior ornamentation of the Temple was consummated while the American mother community was in the throes of the last, most harassing stage of the devastating struggle. The world-wide Centenary celebrations crowning these enterprises were undertaken in such perilous circumstances and carried out despite the formidable obstacles engendered through prolongation of hostilities. National administrative headquarters were established in Ṭihrán, Cairo, Baghdád, Delhi and Sydney, national and international endowments were enriched and assemblies incorporated in countries confronted by growing threat of invasion and encirclement.

The Second Seven Year Plan inaugurating the transatlantic mission embracing Scandinavia, the Low Countries, Switzerland, the Iberian and Italian Peninsulas, was launched on the morrow of the catastrophic upheaval despite the exhaustion, confusion, distress and restrictions afflicting a war-shattered continent. The first fruits of this newly launched Plan were garnered through convocation of first European Teaching Conference and erection of the ninth pillar of the Universal House of Justice in the Dominion of Canada despite premonitory rumblings of a third ordeal threatening to engulf the Eastern and Western Hemispheres. The central structure of the Báb's Sepulcher was built while the precious life of its builder was hanging perilously in the balance. Plans were drawn, contracts placed and foundations laid for its arcade while the holy places were ravaged by flames of the civil strife burning fiercely in the Holy Land.

Precious years are inexorably slipping by. The world outlook is steadily darkening. The American Community's most arduous feats still lie ahead. Disasters overtaking Europe and America, more afflictive than any tribulations yet suffered in either continent, may yet attend still more majestic revelations in the unfoldment of concluding stage of the Second Seven Year Plan destined to witness successively the raising of the tenth and eleventh pillars of the Universal House of Justice, and the celebration of the Golden Jubilee of the Mother Temple of the West.

The champion builders of Bahá'u'lláh's rising World Order must scale nobler heights of heroism as humanity plunges into greater depths of despair, degradation, dissension and distress. Let them forge ahead into the future serenely confident that the hour of their mightiest exertions and the supreme opportunity for their greatest exploits must coincide with the apocalyptic upheaval marking the lowest ebb in mankind's fast-declining fortunes.

[November 3, 1948]

The Citadel of the Faith of Bahá'u'lláh

As the threat of still more violent convulsions assailing a travailing age increases, and the wings of yet another conflict, destined to contribute a distinct, and perhaps a decisive, share to the birth of the new Order which must signalize the advent of the Lesser Peace, darken the international horizon, the eyes of the divers communities, comprising the body of the organized followers of Bahá'u'lláh throughout the Eastern Hemisphere, are being increasingly fixed upon the progressive unfoldment of the tasks which the executors of 'Abdu'l-Bahá's Mandate have been summoned to undertake in the course of the second stage of their world-girdling mission. Past experience, ranging over a period of many years, has taught them that no matter how formidable the external obstacles that have confronted them during the turbulent and eventful decades since the Master's passing, and despite the strain and stress which internal crises, precipitated by enemies from within and by adverse economic circumstances afflicting their country, have imposed, the stalwart occupants of the citadel of the Faith of Bahá'u'lláh have with extraordinary steadfastness, enviable fidelity and magnificent courage, not only shielded the interests, preserved the integrity and demonstrated the worthiness, of the Cause they have embraced, but have sallied forth, with dynamic and irrepressible energy, to implant its banner and establish its outposts in countries and continents far beyond the original scene of their operations.

STAUNCHNESS OF AMERICAN BELIEVERS

Neither the irreparable loss sustained by the termination of the earthly life of a vigilant Master, nor the acute distress caused by the financial collapse which suddenly swept their country, nor the unprecedented tragedy of a world crisis that swept their land and its people into its vortex, nor the perils and uncertainties, the exhaustion and the disillusionment associated with its aftermath nor even the soul-shaking tests which periodically assailed them, through the defection and the attacks of Covenant-breakers, occupying, by virtue of their kinship to, or their long association with, the Founder of their community, exalted positions at the World Center of the Faith, or in the land from which it sprang, or in their own country—none of these have succeeded in vitiating the hidden spring of their spiritual life, in deflecting them from their chosen course, or in even retarding the forward march and fruition of their enterprises. In the toilsome task of fixing the pattern, of laying the foundations, of erecting the machinery, and of setting in operation the Administrative Order of their Faith, in the execution of the successive stages in the erection and exterior ornamentation of their Temple, in the launching of the initial enterprise under 'Abdu'l-Bahá's Divine Plan, which enabled them to establish the structural basis of the Order, recently laid in their homeland, in every republic of Central and South America; in the sustained, the systematic and prodigious effort exerted for the enlargement of the administrative foundations of the institutions of their Faith in every state and province of the United States and the Dominion of Canada; in the parallel endeavors aimed at the widespread dissemination of its literature, and the proclamation of its verities and tenets to the masses; in the launching of the Second Seven Year Plan, which has extended the ramifications of the Divine Plan across the Atlantic to ten sovereign states of the European continent and which has already yielded a rich return through the formation of the first Canadian Bahá'í National Assembly and the convocation of the first European Teaching Conference; in the repeated, the timely, the spontaneous and generous contributions they have made, on numerous occasions, for the relief of the persecuted among their brethren, for the defense of their institutions, for the vindication of their rights, for the consolidation of their activities and the progress of their enterprises—in all these the champions of the Faith of Bahá'u'lláh have, with ever-increasing emphasis, borne witness to the sublimity of the faith which burns within their breasts, to the radiance of the vision that shines clearly and steadily before their eyes, the sureness and rapidity that mark their gigantic strides, and the vastness and glory of the unique mission entrusted to their hands.

Milestones of historic significance have been successively reached and rapidly left behind. A still stonier stretch of road now lies before them. Rumblings of catastrophes yet more dreadful agitate with increasing frequency a sorely stressed and chaotic world, presenting a challenge to grapple with the unfinished tasks, a challenge graver and still more pressing than any hitherto experienced.

PRESS FORWARD ON TEMPLE CONTRACTS

The present and remaining contracts, designed to consummate the magnificent enterprise, initiated almost fifty years ago, in the heart of the North American continent and complete an edifice consecrated for all time by the loving hands of the Center of Bahá'u'lláh's Covenant, constituting the foremost symbol of the Faith, and incarnating the soul of the American Bahá'í Community in the Western Hemisphere, must be speedily and systematically carried out, however onerous the task may become, in consequence of the inevitable fluctuations to which the present economic conditions are subjected, in preparation for the jubilee that must mark the completion of that holy edifice. The recent broadening of the administrative basis of the Faith in a land that has served, and will long remain the base of the spiritual operations now being conducted in both hemispheres, in response to the ringing call of 'Abdu'l-Bahá, sounded three decades ago in His historic Tablets, must, no matter how arduous and insistent the tasks to be performed in Latin America and Europe, be fully maintained, and the process continually enlarged and steadily consolidated. The various agencies designed to carry the Message to the masses, and to present to them befittingly the teachings of its Author, must, likewise, be vigilantly preserved, supported and encouraged. The essential preliminaries, calculated to widen the basis of the forthcoming Latin American national Bahá'í assemblies, to familiarize the Latin American believers with the administrative duties and functions they will be called upon to discharge and to enrich and deepen their knowledge of the essentials of their Faith, its ideals, its history, its requirements and its problems, must be carried out with ever-increasing energy as the hour of the emergence of these Latin American communities into independent existence steadily and inexorably approaches. The necessary guidance, which can alone be properly insured through the maintenance of an uninterrupted extension of administrative assistance, through the settlement of pioneers and the visits of itinerant teachers to the daughter communities, must under no circumstances be completely withdrawn, after their independence has been achieved. Above all, the momentous enterprise initiated in the transatlantic field of service, so vast in conception, so timely, so arduous, so far-reaching in its potentialities, so infinitely meritorious, must in the face of obstacles, however insurmountable they may seem, be continually reinvigorated through undiminished financial support, through an ever-expanding supply of literature in each of the required languages, through frequent, and whenever possible prolonged, visits of itinerant teachers, through the continued settlement of pioneers, through the consolidation of the assemblies already established, through the early constitution of properly functioning assemblies in the few remaining goal countries as yet deprived of this inestimable blessing, and last but not least through the exertion of sustained and concentrated efforts designed to supplement these foci of Bahá'í national administrative activity with subsidiary centers whose formation will herald the inauguration of teaching enterprises throughout the provinces of each of these ten countries.

As the dynamic forces, sweeping forward the First Seven Year Plan, on the last stages of its execution, rose rapidly to a crescendo, culminating in the nationwide celebrations marking the centenary of the Faith of Bahá'u'lláh and synchronized with a further and still more precipitous decline in the fortunes of a war-torn bleeding society, so must every aggravation in the state of a world still harassed by the ravages of a devastating conflict, and now hovering on the brink of a yet more crucial struggle, be accompanied by a still more ennobling manifestation of the spirit of this second crusade, whose consummation might well coincide with a period of distress far more acute than the one through which humanity is now passing.

CEASELESS EFFORT ESSENTIAL

Not ours to speculate, or dwell upon the immediate workings of an inscrutable Providence presiding alike over the falling fortunes of a dying Order and the rising glory of a Plan holding within it the seeds of the world's spiritual revival and ultimate redemption. Nor can we attempt as yet, whilst the second stage in the operation of such a Plan has not yielded its destined fruit, to visualize the nature of the tasks, or discern the character of the circumstances that will mark the progressive unfoldment of a third successive crusade, the successful termination of which must signalize the closing of the first historic epoch in the evolution of the Divine Plan. All we can be sure of, and confidently assert, is that upon the outcome of the assiduous efforts now being collectively exerted, in three continents, by the North American, the Latin and European believers, acting under the Mandate of 'Abdu'l-Bahá, associated with the one and only Plan conceived by Himself, aided by the agencies deriving their inspiration from His Will and Testament, and assured of the support promised by the pen of His Father, in His Most Holy Book, must solely depend the timing as well as the nature of the tasks which must be successfully carried out ere the closing of an epoch of such transcendent brightness and glory in the evolution of the mightiest Plan ever generated through the creative power of the Most Great Name, as manifested by the Will of the Center of His Covenant and the Interpreter of His Teaching.

There can be no doubt whatever that with every turn of the wheel, as a result of the operation of 'Abdu'l-Bahá's Plan, and with every extension in the range of its evolution, a responsibility of still greater gravity and of wider import will have to be shouldered by its divinely chosen executors wherever its ramifications may extend and however oppressive the state of the countries and continents in which they may have to labor. They must strive, ceaselessly strive, ready for any emergency, steeled to meet any degree of opposition, unsatisfied with any measure of progress as yet achieved, prepared to make sacrifices far exceeding any they have already willingly made, and confident that such striving, such readiness, such resolution, such high-mindedness, such sacrifice will earn them the palm of a victory still more soul-satisfying and resounding in its magnificence than any as yet won since the inception of their mission.

May He Who called them into being and raised them up, Who fostered them in their infancy, Who extended to them the blessing of His personal support in their years of childhood, Who bequeathed to them the distinguishing heritage of His Plan, Whose Will and Testament initiated them, during the period of their adolescence, in the processes of a divinely appointed Administrative Order, Who enabled them to attain maturity through the inauguration of the first stage in the execution of His Plan, Who conferred upon them the privilege of spiritual parenthood at the close of the initial phase in the operation of that same Plan, continue through the further unfoldment of the second stage in its evolution to guide their steps along the path leading to the assumption of functions proclaiming the attainment of full spiritual manhood, and enable them eventually, through the long and slow processes of evolution and in conformity with the future requirements of a continually evolving Plan, to manifest before the eyes of the members of their sister communities, their countrymen and the whole world, and in all their plenitude, the potentialities inherent within them, and which in the fullness of time, must reflect in its perfected form, the glories of the mission constituting their birthright.

[November 8, 1948]

Budget Approved for 1949-1950

Approve committing community to amounts proposed for 1949 and 1950 in your letter of November 11. Urgent to curtail if necessary expenditure on Public Relations, National Programming and Radio during the next two years. Ardently praying for solution of problem, removal of difficulties, attainment of high objectives.

[November 25, 1948]

Preliminary Temple Contracts

Welcome preliminary contracts for Temple and determination to ensure completion. Advise drastic reduction in appropriation for activities except budgets for Latin America and European campaign, if maximum sum for Temple is exceeded. Praying for removal of difficulties, continual divine guidance, wise conduct of manifold activities for Faith. Deepest love.

[December 10, 1948]

Arcade for the Shrine of the Báb

Convey to believers the joyful news of the safe delivery on Mt. Carmel of a consignment of thirty-two granite monolith columns, part of the initial shipment of material ordered for construction of the arcade of the Báb's Sepulcher, designed to envelop and preserve the sacred previous structure reared by 'Abdu'l-Bahá. Building operations are soon starting notwithstanding the difficulties of the present situation. I am supplicating the Almighty's guidance and sustaining grace for successive stages of an enterprise envisaged sixty years ago by Bahá'u'lláh, initiated by the Center of His Covenant, designed to culminate as contemplated by Him in erection of a superstructure to be crowned by a golden dome marking the consummation at the heart of the Mountain of God of the momentous undertaking born through the generating influence of the Will of the Founder of our beloved Faith, so dear to the heart of His blessed Son, and dedicated to the memory of the Martyr-Prophet, the immortal Herald of the Bahá'í Dispensation.

[December 13, 1948]

Drastic Budget Reduction

Further drastic reduction in budget for next two years including temporary suspension of Public Relations, National Programming, radio activities; *World Order, Bahá'í World* publications permissible if necessary.

[December 22, 1948]

Further Budget Reduction

Advise plan two. Urge, however, maintain permanent entrance ways, vestibules and metal doors. Also permanent rubber tile or terrazzo floor. Considering soaring prices, shortness of period, weighty issues involved, approve still more drastic reduction of budget, complete suspension during two years of appropriations for activities unconnected with European project, Latin American work and assembly consolidation in United States.

[January 13, 1949]

("*Plan two*" *refers to a series of possible Temple construction schedules submitted to the Guardian.*)

Curtailment of Some Activities

Budgets for activities in Europe, Latin America and consolidation work in United States should not be reduced owing to their vital relation to Second Seven Year Plan. All other activities, whether connected with proclamation of Faith, publications, Bahá'í Magazine, *Bahá'í World* or schools, should either be drastically curtailed or suspended during two years. Holding Annual Convention and maintenance of *Bahá'í News* essential.

[January 19, 1949]

Divert Contributions to Temple Fund

Advise that you divert contributions for International Fund to Temple Fund, and suspend *World Order Magazine*.

[February 26, 1949]

Suspend *World Order Magazine*

Advise you to suspend magazine for next two years. Appeal on my behalf to subscribers in East and West to devote their subscription fee to Temple Fund. Owing to present emergency such action would be highly meritorious.

[February 28, 1949]

A Testing Period Recalling Ordeals of the Dawn-Breakers

The first half of the opening decade of the second Bahá'í century is terminating. The great-minded, stout-hearted, high-spirited American Bahá'í Community, laden with the trophies accumulated in the course of its fifty years' magnificent stewardship of the Faith of Bahá'u'lláh is irresistibly embarking upon a two and a half year period unsurpassed in its fateful consequences by any previous stage traversed in the community's eventful history.

Its members, without exception, are called upon to steel themselves without delay to face an unexpected emergency, seize a God-given opportunity, meet a supreme challenge, and show forth a tenacity of purpose, a solidarity in sacrifice, an austerity in everyday life, worthy the Martyr-Prophet of their Faith as well as their heroic spiritual forebears, the hundredth anniversary of whose agonizing tribulations, including captivity, sieges, betrayals, spoliation and martyrdom, is being commemorated during this same period.

No lesser tribute can be paid the memory of the glorious Báb, the immortal Quddús, the lion-hearted Mullá Husayn, the erudite Vahíd, the audacious Hujjat, the illustrious seven martyrs of Tihrán and a host of unnumbered heroes whose lifeblood flowed so copiously in the course of the opening decade of the first Bahá'í century, by the privileged champion-builders of the World Order of Bahá'u'lláh during the present critical stage in the unfoldment of the Formative Age of His Dispensation, than a parallel outpouring of their substance by the builders of the most holy House of Worship laboring in the corresponding decade of the succeeding century.

The American Bahá'í Community, exalted, singled out among sister communities of East and West through revelation of the Tablets of the Divine Plan, is unavoidably approaching a testing period, crucial, prolonged, potent, purifying, clearly envisaged by 'Abdu'l-Bahá, different from but recalling in its severity the ordeals which afflicted the dawn-breakers in a former Age.

The anticipated trials will enable its members to plumb greater depths of consecration, soar to nobler heights of collective endeavor, and disclose in fuller measure the future glory of their destiny.

Might not the strain, the stress, of the strenuous period now being ushered in through inscrutable dispensations of Providence be productive of perspicuous benefits and blessings reminiscent of the incalculable outpourings of divine grace which followed closely in the train of the woeful trials immortalizing the initial, the bloodiest, the most dramatic period in the Heroic Age of the Bahá'í Dispensation.

[March 16, 1949]

Arcade of the Báb's Shrine Begun

Convey to friends the joyful historic news of commencement of construction of arcade of the Báb's Shrine coinciding with fortieth anniversary of the placing of His remains in marble sarcophagus in vault of the same shrine by 'Abdu'l-Bahá.

[March 21, 1949]

One Remaining Objective Hangs in the Balance

The American Bahá'í Community, undefeated as yet in the performance of any task undertaken collectively by its members, in the course of its eventful history, is now entering a period of grave emergency, that will try the mettle of every single one of its members. Severe as the challenge will be, however prolonged the test, no matter how distracting the condition of the world about them, the issues which claim every ounce of their energy and call for their sustained, wholehearted, concentrated attention are so weighty that none can evaluate at present the influence they will exert on the course of the community's future destiny.

There can be no doubt that the Second Seven Year Plan, the vital link binding the initial and concluding stages of the first epoch in the progressive evolution of 'Abdu'l-Bahá's long-term continually unfolding Plan, has reached its crucial phase—a phase on which hinge the fortunes not only of the Plan itself but of the community as a whole.

The fourth objective of the Plan, the transatlantic project, on which its members have embarked, has, four years ahead of schedule, been, to all intents and purposes, victoriously achieved. The third objective has been partly attained, while its complete fulfillment, as a direct consequence of the marvelous success that has attended the valiant labors of the American pioneers and the newly enrolled native believers in Latin America, appears to be now fully assured. The attainment of the first objective has, as a result of the remarkable impetus given, during the opening years of the Plan, to the multiplication of spiritual assemblies and the proclamation of the Faith in North America, been greatly facilitated, and will, with steady effort, involving not too great an expenditure of energy, be insured in the course of the concluding phase of the Plan. The completion of the Mother Temple of the West, the sacredness of which neither the first Mashriqu'l-Adhkár of the Bahá'í world, nor any future House of Worship to be erected by the followers of Bahá'u'lláh, in any country, at any future date, can rival, in time for the celebration of its Jubilee, is the one remaining objective that now hangs precariously in the balance. Owing to a combination of circumstances wholly beyond the control of its builders, this task has assumed a critical importance, and is of such vital urgency, that no prosecutor of the Plan, eager to witness its consummation, can afford to ignore for a moment.

The sacrifice demanded is such as to have no parallel whatsoever in the history of that community. The manifold issues inextricably interwoven with the campaign audaciously launched for the achievement of this high objective are of such a weighty character as to overshadow every enterprise embarked upon through the organized efforts of its members, in either the concluding years of the Heroic Age of the Faith or the first epoch of the Age which succeeded it. The two years during which this emergency will be most keenly felt coincide on the one hand with a period of increasing distraction occasioned by the uncertainties, the perils and fears of a steadily worsening international situation, and on the other with the centenary of one of the most turbulent, afflictive and glorious stages of Bahá'í history—a stage immortalized by an effusion of blood, a self-abnegation, a heroism unsurpassed not only in the annals of the Faith but in the world's spiritual history. How meritorious, indeed, are the self-denying acts which this supremely challenging hour now calls forth, amidst the perplexities and confusion which present-day society is now experiencing! And yet, how trifling in comparison with the self-immolation of the most distinguished, the most precious heroes and saints of the Primitive Age of our glorious Faith! An outpouring of treasure, no less copious than the blood shed so lavishly in the Apostolic Age of the Faith by those who in the heart of the Asiatic continent proclaimed its birth to the world, can befit their spiritual descendants, who, in the present Formative Age of the Bahá'í Dispensation, have championed the Cause, and assumed so preponderating a share in the erection of its Administrative Order, and are now engaged in the final stage of the building of the House that incarnates the soul of that Faith in the American continent. No sacrifice can be deemed too great to insure the completion of such an edifice—the most holy House of Worship ever to be associated with the Faith of the Most Great Name—an edifice whose inception has shed such a luster on the closing years of the Heroic Age of the Bahá'í Dispensation, which has assumed a concrete shape in the present Formative stage in the evolution of our beloved Faith, whose dependencies must spring into existence in the course of successive epochs of this same Age, and whose fairest fruits will be garnered in the Age that is to come, the last, the Golden Age of the initial and brightest Dispensation of the five-thousand-century Bahá'í Cycle.

"A most wonderful and thrilling motion will appear in the world of existence," are 'Abdu'l-Bahá's own words, predicting the release of spiritual forces that must accompany the completion of this most hallowed House of Worship. "From that point of light," He, further glorifying that edifice, has written, "the spirit of teaching . . . will permeate to all parts of the world." And again: "Out of this Mashriqu'l-Adhkár, without doubt, thousands of Mashriqu'l-Adhkárs will be born." "It marks the inception of the Kingdom of God on earth."

Again I repeat—and I cannot overrate the vital, the unique importance of the campaign now launched to insure the completion of such an edifice—the immediate destiny of the American Bahá'í Community is intimately and inescapably bound up with the outcome of this newly launched, this severely trying, soul-purging, spiritually uplifting campaign. The God-given mission, constituting the birthright, and proclaiming the primacy of a community whose members the Founder of that community, the Center of the Covenant Himself, has addressed as the "Apostles of Bahá'u'lláh," can only be fulfilled if they befittingly obey the specific Mandate issued by 'Abdu'l-Bahá in His Tablets of the Divine Plan. The execution of this Mandate is, in its turn, dependent upon the triumphant conclusion of the Second Seven Year Plan, the second stage in the series of specific plans formulated to insure the successful termination of the opening phase in the execution of that Mandate. Indeed, the successive plans, inaugurated since the birth of the second Bahá'í century, by the British, the Indian, the Persian, the Australia-New Zealand, the 'Iráqí, the German and the Egyptian National Assemblies, with the exception of the plan undertaken by the Canadian National Assembly, which forms an integral part of the Plan associated with the Tablets of 'Abdu'l-Bahá, are but supplements to the vast enterprise whose features have been delineated in those Tablets and are to be regarded, by their very nature, as regional in scope, in contrast with the world-embracing character of the mission entrusted to the community of the champion builders of the World Order of Bahá-'u'lláh, and the torch-bearers of the civilization which that Order must eventually establish. As to the Second Seven Year Plan itself, its eventual success must depend on the attainment of its second and most vital objective. This objective, in its turn, cannot be achieved unless the two-year campaign, now launched by the elected representatives of this community, is successfully carried out. Nor can this campaign yield its richest fruit unless and until the community, in its entirety, participates in this nation-wide sacrificial effort. Nor can this collective effort be blessed, to the fullest extent possible, unless the contributions made by its members involve acts of self-abnegation, not only on the part of those of modest means, but also by those endowed with substantial resources. Nor, indeed, can these self-denying acts, by both the rich and the poor, be productive of the fullest possible benefit unless this sacrificial effort is neither momentary nor haphazard, but rather systematic and continuous throughout the period of the present emergency.

Then and only then will this holy edifice, symbol and harbinger of a world civilization as yet unborn, and the embodiment of the sacrifice of a multitude of the upholders of the Faith of Bahá'u'lláh, release the full measure of the regenerative power with which it has been endowed, shed in all its plenitude the glory of the Most Holy Spirit dwelling within it, and vindicate, beyond the shadow of a doubt, the truth of every single promise recorded by the pen of 'Abdu'l-Bahá pertaining to its destiny.

No more befitting consummation for this magnificent enterprise can be envisaged than that this noble edifice, whose cornerstone has been laid by 'Abdu'l-Bahá's own hands, the preliminary measure for whose construction synchronized with the formal interment of the Báb's remains on Mt. Carmel, within whose walls the first Centenary of the birth of His ministry has been celebrated, whose interior ornamentation has coincided with the construction of the arcade of His Sepulcher, should be vouchsafed the honor of having the Jubilee of its inception coincide with, and celebrated on the occasion of, the Centenary of the birth of Bahá'u'lláh's prophetic Mission in the Síyáh-Chál of Ṭihrán.

[April 11, 1949]

Process of Expansion Accelerates

[MESSAGE TO 1949 CONVENTION]

Desire to share with attendants at Forty-first American Bahá'í Convention feelings of joyous gratitude evoked by the steady acceleration of the dual process of expansion and consolidation of the Bahá'í World Community as well as the perspicuous evidences of divine protection vouchsafed the World Center of the Faith during the course of the third year of the Second Seven Year Plan. The number of countries included within the pale of the Faith is ninety-four. Languages into which Bahá'í literature is translated, and assemblies, local and national, incorporated, now total fifty-six and one hundred five, respectively. Bahá'í literature now being translated into fourteen additional languages. The number of centers in Latin America is one hundred and nine. The fourth objective of the present Plan has been achieved four years ahead of schedule through the formation of a spiritual assembly in each of the ten goal countries on the European continent. Centers established in these countries total thirty-one, newly enrolled native believers, one hundred fifty-four. Nearly a million dollar drive to complete the Mother Temple of the West has been auspiciously launched and construction of interior sections of the ornamentation initiated. Number of settlements in Greenland provided with Bahá'í scriptures raised to forty-eight, including Thule beyond the Arctic Circle and Etah near eightieth latitude. Number of

American states, territories and federal districts recognizing Bahá'í marriage raised to eighteen. Restoration of the newly acquired German national Ḥaẓíratu'l-Quds at Frankfurt has been commenced. Formulation of five year plans for German and Egyptian National Assemblies, culminating at the Centenary of the Birth of Bahá'u'lláh's prophetic Mission, completes the number of national assemblies pledged to achieve within appointed time specified goals in five continents. The European Teaching Conference convened at Geneva inaugurating series of annual gatherings designed to consolidate the tremendously significant transatlantic project. Bahá'í observers accredited by United Nations participated in Conference on Human Rights, Geneva; United Nations General Assembly, Paris. Bahá'í representative attended Luxembourg general conference of world movement for world federation. First all red Indian Assembly consolidated at Macy, Nebraska. Building operations on arcade of Báb's Sepulcher commenced forty years after official interment of His remains by 'Abdu'l-Bahá. Prolonged hostilities ravaging Holy Land providentially terminated. Bahá'í holy places, unlike those belonging to other faiths, miraculously safeguarded. Perils no less grave than those which threatened the World Center of the Faith under 'Abdu'l-Ḥamíd and Jamál Páshá and through Hitler's intended capture of the Near East, averted. Independent sovereign state within confines of Holy Land established and recognized, marking termination of twenty-century-long provincial status. Formal assurance of the protection of Bahá'í holy sites and continuation of Bahá'í pilgrimage given by Prime Minister of newly emerged state. Official invitation extended by its government on the historic occasion of the opening of the state's first parliament. Official record of Bahá'í marriage endorsed, Bahá'í endowments exempted by responsible authorities of the same state. Best wishes for the future welfare of the Faith of Bahá'u'lláh conveyed in writing by the newly elected head of the state in reply to congratulatory message addressed him upon assumption of his office. Appeal to entire community, through assembled delegates, in thankful recognition of the manifold blessings vouchsafed the Faith and in response to the alert sounded for the present emergency, to arise and demonstrate more conspicuously than ever before, through greater austerity at home and increasing audacity in foreign fields, both in Latin America and Europe, their grim determination at whatever cost, no matter how crucial the test, however long the period, however herculean the labor, to carry forward unremittingly their task to its triumphant conclusion.

[April 25, 1949]

Welcome Initial Victory

Greatly welcome, much impressed by remarkable feat of initial victory collectively achieved by self-sacrificing efforts of invincible, far-visioned, forward-marching American Bahá'í Community. Ultimate victory now in sight bidding fair to bring present emergency period to triumphant conclusion, seal fate of Second Seven Year Plan and open prospect of glorious inauguration at appointed time of third collective Plan designed to terminate initial chapter in story of mysterious unfoldment of Divine Plan. Rejoice particularly at formulation of teaching plans so vitally linked with immediate destiny of Temple enterprise. Owing to relaxation of pressure occasioned by critical situation advise direct special attention to invigorate activities conducted in Latin America and European continent. Need for voluntary, self-supporting, wholly dedicated pioneers calculated to supplement newly launched undertaking in both fields is still pressing and acquiring greater urgency owing to approaching emergence of Latin American national assemblies and necessity to consolidate swiftly the newly-formed local assemblies in ten European goal countries. Heart uplifted at contemplation of mighty range of accomplishments embracing so vast a field in both hemispheres. Prayers continually ascending to Abhá throne both in thanksgiving for marvelous bounties already vouchsafed and in supplication for renewal of strength for attainment of future goals.

[June 29, 1949]

Supplicating Blessing for American Activities

Delighted by progress of Temple work. Highly approve, deeply appreciate suggestion to defray expenses of German representative to Brussels conference. Supplicating Almighty's blessing for manifold activities pursued, unrelaxing vigilance, unflinching determination, exemplary self-sacrifice in three continents by divinely sustained American Bahá'í Community.

[July 20, 1949]

Corners of Shrine Arcade Under Construction

Inform friends of commencement of construction on three corners of arcade of Shrine. Six granite pilasters already erected, twelve columns will be raised shortly. Forwarding photographs for publicity purposes.

[August 7, 1949]

This Hour, Crowded With Destiny

The efforts exerted, and the results achieved, by the members of the American Bahá'í Community during the opening months of the two-year emergency period are such as to merit the highest commendation and praise. They will, if the effort be sustained, evoke the admiration of the entire Bahá'í world, which is now watching, with feelings of wonder and expectancy, the outcome of the tremendous labor of this community now confronted with one of the most challenging, arduous and far-reaching tasks ever undertaken in its history.

The great forward stride that has already been undertaken, during so short a period, augurs well for the ultimate victory, now within sight—a victory which will pave the way for the successful execution of a seven-year enterprise, destined, in its turn, to enable its executors to launch, at the appointed time, the third and most glorious stage in the initial unfoldment of 'Abdu'l-Bahá's unique and grand design for that privileged and conspicuously blessed community.

No less striking has been the achievement of the representatives of this community in the vast and most recent field of their historic and highly meritorious endeavors, exerted beyond the confines of their homeland, where over so vast a territory, on a continent so agitated, and amidst peoples so disillusioned, so varied in race, language and outlook, so impoverished spiritually, so paralyzed with fear, so confused in thought, so abased in their moral standards, so rent by internal schisms, victories so rich in promise, so startling in their rapidity, so magnificent in their range, have been won, and ennobled, to such a marked degree, the deathless record of American Bahá'í service to the Faith of Bahá'u'lláh.

Now that so prodigious and successful an effort has been exerted on behalf of the historic and sacred Temple, whose completion constitutes so vital an objective of the Second Seven Year Plan, and so conspicuous a triumph won in the transatlantic sphere of its operation, its needs and other vital objectives, both at home and in the Latin American field, must receive, in the months immediately ahead, the particular attention of both the national elected representatives of the community who supervise the working of the Plan and the mass of believers who participate in its execution.

While the financial requirements of the Mother Temple of the West are being met with unabated heroism by rich and poor alike in the critical months that lie ahead, and the measures to ensure the undiminished support, and the uninterrupted consolidation of the European enterprise are being assiduously carried out, a parallel effort, no less strenuous and sustained should be simultaneously exerted in the North American continent and in Central and South America, for the purpose of preserving the prizes already won over the length and breadth of the Western Hemisphere, where the initial impulse of this mighty and Divine Plan has been felt and its initial victories in foreign fields registered.

The assemblies of the North American continent, constituting the base for the gigantic operations destined to warm and illuminate, under American Bahá'í auspices, the five continents of the globe, must, at no time and under no circumstances, be allowed to diminish in number or decline in strength and in influence. The movement of pioneers, whether settlers or itinerant teachers, which in fields so distant from this base, has exhibited so marvelous a vitality, must, within the limits of the homeland itself, be neither interrupted nor suffer a decline. The groups and isolated centers so painstakingly formed and established must, conjointly with this highly commendable and essential duty, be maintained, fostered and if possible multiplied.

No less attention, while this emergency period taxes, to an unprecedented degree, the combined resources of the envied trustees of

'Abdu'l-Bahá's Divine Plan, should be directed to the vast network of
Bahá'í enterprises initiated throughout Latin America, where the work
so nobly conceived, so diligently prosecuted, so conspicuously blessed,
is rapidly nearing the first stage of its fruition. The flow of pioneers, so
vital in all its aspects, and which has yielded such inestimable benefits
at the early stages of this widely ramified enterprise, must, however
urgent the other tasks already shouldered by an overburdened yet
unfailingly protected community, be neither arrested nor slacken. The
outpost of the newly born communities, established in the Straits of
Magallanes in the South, must be held with undiminished vigor and
determination. The major task of ensuring the breadth and solidity of
the foundations laid for the establishment of two national Bahá'í
assemblies, through the preservation of the present assemblies, groups
and isolated centers, and the restoration of any of these vital centers,
now dissolved, to their former status, must be scrupulously watched
and constantly encouraged. The process of the dissemination of Bahá'í
literature, of Bahá'í publication and translation, must continue unabated, however much the sacrifice involved. The newly fledged institutions of teaching and regional committees, of summer schools and of
congresses, must be continually encouraged and increasingly supported
by teachers as well as administrators, by pioneers from abroad, as well as
by the native believers themselves. The highly salutary and spiritually
beneficent experiment of encouraging a more active participation by
these newly won supporters of the Faith in Latin America, and a
greater assumption of administrative responsibility on their part, in the
ever expanding activities to be entrusted wholly to their care in the
years to come, should be, in particular, developed, systematized and
placed on a sure and unassailable foundation. Above all, the paramount
duty of deepening the spiritual life of these newly fledged, these
precious and highly esteemed co-workers, and of enlightening their
minds regarding the essential verities enshrined in their Faith, its
fundamental institutions, its history and genesis—the twin Covenants
of Bahá'u'lláh and of 'Abdu'l-Bahá, the present Administrative Order,
the future World Order, the Laws of the Most Holy Book, the
inseparable institutions of the Guardianship and of the Universal
House of Justice, the salient events of the Heroic and Formative Ages
of the Faith, and its relationship with the Dispensations that have
preceded it, its attitude toward the social and political organizations by

which it is surrounded—must continue to constitute the most vital aspect of the great spiritual Crusade launched by the champions of the Faith from among the peoples of their sister republics in the South.

The magnitude of the tasks these heroes and champions of the Faith are summoned, at this hour, crowded with destiny, to discharge from the borders of Greenland to the southern extremity of Chile in the Western Hemisphere, and from Scandinavia in the north, to the Iberian peninsula in the south of the European continent, is, indeed, breath-taking in its implications and back-breaking in the strain it imposes. The sacrifices they are called upon to voluntarily make for the successful performance of such herculean, such holy, such epoch-making tasks, are comparable to none but those which their spiritual forbears have willingly accepted at the hour of the birth of their Faith more than a hundred years ago. Theirs is the privilege, no less meritorious and perhaps as epoch-making, to preside, in their own homeland and its neighboring continents, over, and direct the forces generated by, the birth of an order that posterity will acclaim as both the offspring of that Faith, and the precursor of the Golden Age in which that same Faith must, in the fullness of time, find its fullest expression and most glorious consummation.

How great the opportunity which the present hour, so dark in the fortunes of mankind and yet so bright in the ever-unfolding history of their Faith, offers them. How unspeakably precious the reward which they who serve it will reap! How pitiful and urgent the need of the waiting multitudes of these continents, summoned to sustain the initial impact of the operation of a divinely impelled Plan which no force can resist and no power can rival!

For what this superbly equipped community, this irresistibly advancing army of the chosen warriors of Bahá'u'lláh, battling under His banner, operating in conformity with the explicit Mandate voiced by His beloved Son, has already achieved, over so extensive a field, in such a brief time, at such great sacrifice, for so precious a Cause, and in the course of such turbulent years, I cannot but feel the deepest sense of gratitude the like of which no achievement, single or collective, rendered in any other part of the globe, by any community associated with the Cause of the Most Great Name has evoked. For what it will and must achieve in the future I entertain feelings of warm expectation and serene confidence. For it, I will continue, from the depths of a loving and grateful heart to supplicate blessings immeasurably richer than any it has yet experienced.

[August 18, 1949]

Praying For Increasing Success

Delighted at progress of Temple work; urge uninterrupted reinforcement of Latin American and European enterprises through steady flow of pioneers, continued self-sacrifice; praying for increasing success of your high endeavors. Deepest loving appreciation.

[November 6, 1949]

Majesty of the Báb's Shrine Unfolding

Announce to the friends that six hundred tons of stones destined for the arcade of the Báb's Shrine, received in successive shipments to the Holy Land, have been safely transported to its precincts despite repeated accidents—the sinking of a lighter in the harbor and outbreak of fire in the hold of the ship. An additional two hundred tons of material including carved marble mosaic have been ordered through recent contract for erection of parapet designed to crown the columns and arches of the arcade. North and east sides of structure with three corners virtually completed. Construction of cornice and roof, last stage in erection of the arcade, will soon be undertaken. Majesty and beauty of the colonnade enveloping the central holy edifice built by 'Abdu'l-Bahá's hands steadily unfolding, presaging revelation of the full glory of the completed Sepulcher manifesting the plenitude of the splendor of the constructed dome.

[November 13, 1949]

Faithless Brother Hussein

Faithless brother Hussein, already abased through dishonorable conduct over period of years followed by association with Covenant-breakers in Holy Land and efforts to undermine Guardian's position, recently further demeaned himself through marriage under obscure circumstances with lowborn Christian girl in Europe. This disgraceful alliance, following four successive marriages by sisters and cousins with three sons of Covenant-breaker denounced repeatedly by 'Abdu'l-Bahá as His enemy, and daughter of notorious political agitator, brands them with infamy greater than any associated with marriages contracted by old Covenant-breakers whether belonging to family of Muḥammad-'Alí or Badí'u'lláh.

[December 19, 1949]

Maintain Momentum in Triple Field

Delighted by progress in Latin-American field, Temple construction and publicity activities. Announce arrival of first shipment of parapet panels. Anticipate early completion of eastern façade of Shrine including mosaic panels. Urge maintenance of momentum in triple field, home, intercontinental enterprises. Praying for bountiful blessings from the Almighty.

[February 25, 1950]

Shrine Parapet Completed

Announce to the friends the completion, on the eve of Naw-Rúz, of the erection of parapet crowning the eastern façade of Holy Shrine one year after placing the first threshold stones upon the foundation of the arcade. The beauty and majesty of the finely carved panels surmounting the soaring arches spanning the rosy monolith columns, emblazoned with emerald green and scarlet mosaic symbolizing the Báb's lineage and martyrdom, are strikingly revealed. The original pearl-like structure raised by the hands of the Center of the Covenant, enshrining the remains of the Martyr-Prophet of the Faith, acquiring, through construction of the shell designed for its embellishment and preservation, additional height by one-third, additional width by one-fifth, enhancing the massiveness of the edifice embosomed in the Mountain of God, heralding the erection of the lofty gilded dome that will eventually shine forth in solitary splendor from its heart.

[March 21, 1950]

Sacred Task of Present Hour

Approved recommendation regarding treatment of walls. Meeting deficit budget must have precedence over purchase of land near Ḥaẓíra owing to critical situation in Latin America and vital needs in Europe. Steady flow of pioneers to both continents is the imperative, urgent, sacred task of the present hour.

[March 29, 1950]

Shrine Arcade Nearing Completion

Announce to friends that central panel of north façade, adorned with green mosaic with gilded Greatest Name, the fairest gem set in crown of arcade of Shrine, clearly visible from city by day, floodlit by night, is now in position.

Three corner panels bearing symbol of ringstone erected, presaging completion of both parapet and arcade on the occasion of approaching Centenary of martyrdom of the Blessed Báb.

[June 17, 1950]

Centenary of the Martyrdom of the Báb

Moved to share with assembled representatives of American Bahá'í Community gathered beneath the dome of the Most Holy House of Worship in the Bahá'í world, feelings of profound emotion evoked by this historic occasion of the world-wide commemoration of the First Centenary of the Martyrdom of the Blessed Báb, Prophet and Herald of the Faith of Bahá'u'lláh, Founder of the Dispensation marking the culmination of the six thousand year old Adamic Cycle, Inaugurator of the five thousand century Bahá'í Cycle.

Poignantly call to mind the circumstances attending the last act consummating the tragic ministry of the Master-Hero of the most sublime drama in the religious annals of mankind, signalizing the most dramatic event of the most turbulent period of the Heroic Age of the Bahá'í Dispensation, destined to be recognized by posterity as the most precious, momentous sacrifice in the world's spiritual history. Recall the peerless tributes paid to His memory by the Founder of the Faith, acclaiming Him Monarch of God's Messengers, the Primal Point round Whom the realities of all the Prophets circle in adoration. Profoundly stirred by the memory of the agonies He suffered, the glad-tidings He announced, the warnings He uttered, the forces He set in motion, the adversaries He converted, the disciples He raised up, the conflagrations He precipitated, the legacy He left of faith and courage, the love He inspired. Acknowledge with bowed head, joyous, thankful heart the successive, marvelous evidence of His triumphant power in the course of the hundred years elapsed since the last crowning act of His meteoric ministry.

The creative energies released at the hour of the birth of His Revelation, endowing mankind with the potentialities of the attainment of maturity are deranging, during the present transitional age, the equilibrium of the entire planet as the inevitable prelude to the consummation in world unity of the coming of age of the human race. The portentous but unheeded warnings addressed to kings, princes, ecclesiastics are responsible for the successive overthrow of fourteen monarchies of East and West, the collapse of the institution of the Caliphate, the virtual extinction of the Pope's temporal sovereignty, the progressive decline in the fortunes of the ecclesiastical hierarchies of the Islámic, Christian, Jewish, Zoroastrian, and Hindu Faiths.

The Order eulogized and announced in His writings, whose laws Bahá'u'lláh subsequently revealed in the Most Holy Book, whose features 'Abdu'l-Bahá delineated in His Testament, is now passing through its embryonic stage through the emergence of the initial institutions of the world Administrative Order in the five continents of the globe. The clarion call sounded in the Qayyúmu'l-Asmá', summoning the peoples of the West to forsake their homes and proclaim His message, was nobly answered by the communities of the Western Hemisphere headed by the valorous, stalwart American believers, the chosen vanguard of the all-conquering, irresistibly marching army of the Faith in the western world.

The embryonic Faith, maturing three years after His martyrdom, traversing the period of infancy in the course of the Heroic Age of the Faith is now steadily progressing towards maturity in the present Formative Age, destined to attain full stature in the Golden Age of the Bahá'í Dispensation.

Lastly the Holy Seed of infinite preciousness, holding within itself incalculable potentialities representing the culmination of the centuries-old process of the evolution of humanity through the energies released by the series of progressive Revelations starting with Adam and concluded by the Revelation of the Seal of the Prophets, marked by the successive appearance of the branches, leaves, buds, blossoms and plucked, after six brief years by the hand of destiny, ground in the mill of martyrdom and oppression but yielding the oil whose first flickering light cast upon the somber, subterranean walls of the Síyáh-Chál of Tihrán, whose fire gathered brilliance in Baghdád and shone in full resplendency in its crystal globe in Adrianople, whose rays warmed and illuminated the fringes of the American, European, Australian continents through the tender ministerings of the Center of the Covenant, whose radiance is now overspreading the surface of the globe during the present Formative Age, whose full splendor is destined in the course of future milleniums to suffuse the entire planet.

Already the crushing of this God-imbued kernel upon the anvil of adversity has ignited the first sparks of the Holy Fire latent within it through the emergence.of the firmly knit world-encompassing community constituting no less than twenty-five hundred centers established throughout a hundred countries representing over thirty races and extending as far north as the Arctic Circle and as far south as the Straits of Magallanes, equipped with literature translated into sixty languages and possessing endowments nearing ten million dollars, enriched through the erection of two Houses of Worship in the heart of the Asiatic and North American continents and the stately mausoleum reared in its World Center, consolidated through the incorporation of over a hundred of its national and local assemblies and reinforced through the proclamation of its independence in the East, its recognition in the West, eulogized by royalty, buttressed by nine pillars sustaining the future structure of its supreme administrative council, energized through the simultaneous prosecution of specific plans conducted under the aegis of its national councils designed to enlarge the limits and extend the ramifications and consolidate the foundations of its divinely appointed Administrative Order over the surface of the entire planet.

I appeal on this solemn occasion, rendered doubly sacred through the approaching hundredth anniversary of the most devastating holocaust in the annals of the Faith, at this anxious hour in the fortunes of this travailing age, to the entire body of the American believers, the privileged occupants and stout-hearted defenders of the foremost citadel of the Faith, to rededicate themselves and resolve, no matter how great the perils confronting their sister communities on the European, Asiatic, African and Australian continents, however somber the situation facing both the cradle of the Faith and its World Center, however grievous the vicissitudes they themselves may eventually suffer, to hold aloft unflinchingly the torch of the Faith impregnated with the blood of innumerable martyrs and transmit it unimpaired so that it may add luster to future generations destined to labor after them.

[July 4, 1950]

A Worthy, Five-Fold Offering

The first half of the two-year austerity period, inaugurated at so anxious an hour in the fortunes of the Second Seven Year Plan, has been successfully traversed, and deserves to be regarded as a memorable episode in the history of the Faith and the unfoldment of the Plan in the North American continent. An effort, prodigious, nation-wide, sustained, and reminiscent in its heroism and consecration of the immortal exploits of the dawn-breakers of the Apostolic Age of the Bahá'í Dispensation, has been exerted by their spiritual descendants, in circumstances which, though totally different in character, are yet no less challenging and for a cause as meritorious—an effort that has indeed outshone the high endeavors that have distinguished for so long the record of service associated with the American Bahá'í Community. All of its members who have participated in this collective undertaking should be heartily congratulated, particularly those who, by their acts of self-abnegation, have emulated the example of the heroes of our Faith at the early dawn of its history. The entire Bahá'í world is stirred when contemplating the range of such an effort, the depth of consecration reached by those who have participated in it, the results it has achieved, the noble purpose it has served. My heart overflows with gratitude for the repeated evidences of worthiness demonstrated by this generous-hearted, valiant and dedicated community which has, no matter how onerous the task, how challenging the issue, how distracting the external circumstances with which it has been surrounded, never shirked its duty or hesitated for a moment.

The high watermark of so gigantic an exertion, however, still remains to be reached. The year now entered, ushered in and conse-crated by the Centenary of the tragic execution of the Martyr-Prophet of our Faith, and packed with poignant memories of the persecutions of Zanján which stained its history a hundred years ago and carried its fortunes to almost its lowest ebb, and were a prelude to the most ghastly holocaust ever experienced by its followers, must witness as it rolls forward to its close, a still more striking demonstration of the tenacity of the members of this community, a still nobler display of acts of self-sacrifice, a still more inspiring manifestation of solidarity, and evi-dences of a grimmer determination, of a greater courage and persever-ance in response to the triple call of this present hour.

The vital needs of the most holy House of Worship reared in the service and for the glory of the Most Great Name, though virtually met, still require the last exertions to ensure its completion as the hour of its Jubilee approaches. The Latin-American enterprise, initiated thirteen years ago, and marking the initial collective undertaking launched by the American Bahá'í Community beyond the confines of the great republic of the West, and under the mandate of 'Abdu'l-Bahá's Divine Plan, still in a state of emergency and rapidly advancing towards its initial fruition, demands unrelaxing vigilance, and calls for still more strenuous exertions and self-sacrifice on the part of those who have so enthusiastically embarked upon it, who have so conscientiously and painstakingly shepherded it along its destined course and through-out the early stages of its unfoldment, and who are now, as a result of their ceaseless exertions, witnessing the first efflorescence of their mammoth pioneer labors. The construction of the superstructure of the Holy Sepulcher of the Blessed Báb, now, at this anxious and urgent hour, superimposed on the manifold responsibilities shouldered by members of the American Bahá'í Community, affording them the first historic opportunity of directly sustaining, through their contributions, the most sacred enterprise ever undertaken in the history of the Faith, the first and most holy edifice reared at its World Center, and the initial international institution heralding the establishment of the supreme legislative body at the World Administrative Center, requires the immediate and sustained attention of the members of a community whose destiny has been linked, ever since its inception, with the various stages marking the rise and consolidation of this divinely appointed, unspeakably holy enterprise.

An Hour Laden with Fate

The hour is critical, laden with fate. Responsibilities numerous and varied, as well as urgent and sacred, are crowding, in quick succession, upon a community youthful and valorous in spirit, rich in experience, triumphant in the past, sensible of its future obligations, keenly aware of the sublimity of its world mission, inflexibly resolved to follow with unfaltering steps the road of its destiny. The world situation is perilous and gloomy. Rumblings from far and near bode evil for the immediate fortunes of a sadly distracted society. The Second Seven Year Plan is now approaching its conclusion. The Centenary of the Martyrdom of the Báb with all its poignant memories is upon us. We are entering a period crowded with the centenaries of the direst calamities—massacres, sieges, captivities, spoliations and tortures involving thousands of heroes—men, women and children—the world's greatest Faith has ever experienced. Another centenary commemorating an event as tragic and infinitely more glorious is fast approaching. Time is short. Opportunities, though multiplying with every passing hour, will not recur, some for another century, others never again. However severe the challenge, however multiple the tasks, however short the time, however somber the world outlook, however limited the material resources of a hard-pressed adolescent community, the untapped sources of celestial strength from which it can draw are measureless, in their potencies, and will unhesitatingly pour forth their energizing influences if the necessary daily effort be made and the required sacrifices be willingly accepted.

Nor should it be forgotten that in the hour of adversity and in the very midst of confusion, peril and uncertainty, some of the most superb exploits, noising abroad the fame of this community have been achieved. The construction of the superstructure of the Mashriqu'l-Adhkár during one of the severest depressions experienced by the people of the United States in this century; the inauguration of the first Seven Year Plan on the eve of and during the anxious years preceding the second world conflagration; its vigorous prosecution during its darkest days and its triumph before its conclusion; the launching of the European campaign on the morrow of the most devastating conflict that rocked the continent of Europe to its foundation—these stand out as shining evidences of the unfailing protection, guidance and sustaining power vouchsafed its members, so readily and so abundantly, in the hour of their greatest need and danger.

To consolidate the victories won, and reinforce the foundations of the unnumbered institutions so diligently established, in the North American continent; to rear the twin pillars of the Universal House of Justice in Latin America, with their concomitant administrative agencies functioning in no less than twenty republics of Central and South America; to maintain in their present strength the strongholds of the Faith in the ten goal countries of Europe; to complete the interior ornamentation of the first Mashriqu'l-Adhkár of the West, and its Mother Temple, in preparation of its Jubilee; to assist in the erection of the superstructure of a still holier edifice, envisaged by its Founder and established by the Center of His Covenant on God's holy mountain, at the very heart and center of our beloved Faith, would indeed constitute, by virtue of their scope, origin and character, embracing three continents and including within their range the World Center of the Faith itself, a worthy, befitting five-fold offering placed on the altar of the Faith of Bahá'u'lláh, on the occasion of the Centenary of the birth of His Mission by a community which, more than any sister community, in East or West, has contributed, since the inception of the Formative Age of His Faith to the enlargement of its limits, the rise and establishment of its Administrative Order and the spread of its fame, glory and power.

That this community may, in the course of these three coming years, discharge its five-fold task—now assuming, through the stress of circumstances, still vaster proportions, and investing itself with still greater blessedness and merit, than originally envisaged—with a spirit outshining any hitherto shown in the course of its half-century stewardship to the Faith of Bahá'u'lláh, is my most fervent wish and the object of my special and ardent prayers at this time when my heart and mind are fixed upon the sufferings and passion of the Báb on the occasion of the Centenary of His Martyrdom.

[July 5, 1950]

Ruhi and Family Show Open Defiance

Inform friends that Ruhi, his mother, with Ruha, his aunt, and their families, not content with years of disobedience and unworthy conduct, are now showing open defiance. Confident that exemplary loyalty of American believers will sustain me in carrying overwhelming burden of cares afflicting me.

[July 15, 1950]

Non-Bahá'í Gifts

All gifts by non-Bahá'ís are to be used for charity only.

[July 24, 1950]

Teaching in Africa

Feel moved to appeal to gallant, great-hearted American Bahá'í Community to arise on the eve of launching the far-reaching, historic campaign by sister Community of the British Isles to lend valued assistance to the meritorious enterprise undertaken primarily for the illumination of the tribes of East and West Africa, envisaged in the Tablets of the Center of the Covenant revealed in the darkest hour of His ministry.

I appeal particularly to its dearly beloved members belonging to the Negro race to participate in the contemplated project marking a significant milestone in the world-unfoldment of the Faith, supplementing the work initiated fifty years ago on the North American continent, forging fresh links binding the American, British and Egyptian Communities and providing the prelude to the full-scale operations destined to be launched at a later period of the unfoldment of the Divine Plan aiming at the conversion of the backward, oppressed masses of the swiftly awakening continent.

Though such participation is outside the scope of the Second Seven Year Plan, I feel strongly that the assumption of this added responsibility for this distant vital field at this crucial challenging hour, when world events are moving steadily towards a climax and the Centenary of the birth of Bahá'u'lláh's Mission is fast approaching, will further ennoble the record of the world-embracing tasks valiantly undertaken by the American Bahá'í Community and constitute a worthy response to 'Abdu'l-Bahá's insistent call raised on behalf of the race He repeatedly blessed and loved so dearly and for whose illumination He ardently prayed and for whose future He cherished the brightest hopes.

[August 5, 1950]

Comforted by Messages of Devotion

My anguished heart is comforted by the unnumbered messages from communities, assemblies, groups, committees and individual American believers, replete with expressions of loving devotion, pledges of loyalty to 'Abdu'l-Bahá's Covenant, prayers on my behalf and assurances of rededication in service to the precious Faith.

The triple cord binding me to the American Community, outstanding in its affectionate and unfailing support in the course of my almost thirty years' stewardship to the Faith of Bahá'u'lláh, is greatly reinforced. But for America's multitudinous services and unparalleled record of achievements my burden of cares both past and present would be unbearable.

Far from complaining of the added weight of afflictions oppressing me at this hour I feel I cannot but welcome with feelings of thankfulness and humility such tribulations enabling me to taste the cup the Martyr-Prophet of our beloved Faith drained so heroically a hundred years ago.

Much as I desire to acknowledge separately all messages I regretfully find the task beyond the limits of my overtaxed strength. I ask, dearly beloved friends, to regard this message as addressed to each one personally, bearing to each and every one assurance of my constant awareness of their enfolding love and unfailing support as well as my everlasting gratitude and unalterable affection and immense pride in their unrivaled collective share in the world-wide furtherance of the Cause so dear, so precious to us all.

[September 12, 1950]

Relieved by Intensified Activity

My heart is greatly relieved by the splendid, welcome evidences of the intensified activity on the home front, Europe and Latin America. Supplicating bountiful blessings on the manifold enterprises energetically and devotedly conducted by the exemplary American Bahá'í Community.

[September 19, 1950]

Badí'u'lláh Has Miserably Perished

Badí'u'lláh, brother and chief lieutenant of archbreaker of divine Covenant, has miserably perished after sixty years' ceaseless, fruitless efforts to undermine the divinely-appointed Order, having witnessed within the last five months the deaths of his nephews Shoa and Musa, notorious standard-bearers of the rebellion associated with the name of their perfidious father.

[November 3, 1950]

Requirements for Temple Completion

Temple not regarded as completed until all accessories are provided, including landscape gardening. Public announcement and worship must coincide with termination of plan.

[November 8, 1950]

Summer Schools to Reopen

Owing to paramount need of Shrine and Temple, advise that you postpone publication of magazine until 1953. Summer schools may be reopened.

[December 8, 1950 (Excerpt)]

Assistance to Epoch-Making Enterprise in Africa

Assistance to Africa project through financial contribution, participation of pioneers white and colored, and close consultation and cooperation with British Assembly necessary. Independent campaign not intended. Fervently praying the participation of British, American, Persian, and Egyptian National Assemblies in unique, epoch-making enterprise in African continent may prove prelude to convocation of first African Teaching Conference leading eventually to initiation of undertakings involving collaboration among all national assemblies of Bahá'í world, thereby paving way to ultimate organic union of these assemblies through formation of International House of Justice destined to launch enterprises embracing whole Bahá'í world. Acclaim simultaneous inauguration of crusade linking administrative machinery of four national assemblies of East and West within four continents and birth of first International Council at World Center of Faith, twin evidences of resistless unfoldment of embryonic, divinely appointed World Order of Bahá'u'lláh.

[January 17, 1951]

Status of Bahá'ís Regarding Military Duty

No change whatsoever in status of Bahá'ís in relation to active military duty. No compromise of spiritual principles of Faith possible, however tense the situation, however aroused public opinion.

[January 17, 1951]

Spiritual Conquest of the Planet

The virtual termination of the interior ornamentation of the first Mashriqu'l-Adhkár of the West; the forthcoming formation of the twin national spiritual assemblies of Latin America, following upon the establishment of a corresponding institution in the Dominion of Canada; the full attainment of the prescribed goals on the European continent in accordance with the provisions of the Second Seven Year Plan and the consolidation already achieved in the North American continent, do not, under any circumstances, imply that the vast responsibilities, shouldered by a valiant, an alert and resolute community, have been fully and totally discharged, or that its members can afford, as the plan draws to its conclusion, to sink into complacency or relax for one moment in their high endeavors.

The hour destined to mark the triumphant conclusion of the second stage in their historic, divinely conferred, world-encircling mission has not yet struck. Rumblings, loud and persistent, presaging a crisis of extreme severity in world affairs, confront them with a challenge which, in spite of what they have already accomplished, they cannot and must not either ignore or underrate. The rise of the World Administrative Center of their Faith, within the precincts and under the shadow of its World Spiritual Center, a process that has been kept in abeyance for well nigh thirty years, whilst the machinery of the national and local institutions of a nascent Order was being erected and perfected, presents them with an opportunity which, as the champion-builders of that Order and the torchbearers of an as yet unborn civilization, they must seize with alacrity, resolution and utter consecration. The initiation of momentous projects in other continents of the globe, and particularly in Africa, as a result of the growing initiative and the spirit of enterprise exhibited by their fellow-workers in East and West, cannot leave unmoved the vanguard of a host summoned by 'Abdu'l-Bahá, its Divine Commander, and in accordance with the provisions of a God-given Charter, to play such a preponderating role in the spiritual conquest of the entire planet. Above all, the rapid prosecution of an enterprise transcending any undertaking, whether national or local, embarked upon by the followers of the Faith of Bahá'u'lláh, destined to attain its consummation with the erection of the dome of the Báb's holy Sepulcher, imposes an added obligation, owing to unforeseen circumstances, on the already multitudinous duties assumed by a community wholly absorbed in the various tasks it shoulders. In fact, as the Centenary of the birth of Bahá'u'lláh's prophetic Mission approaches, His American followers, not content with the successful conclusion, in their entirety, of the tasks assigned to them, must aspire to celebrate befittingly this historic occasion, as becomes the chosen recipients, and the privileged trustees, of a divinely conceived Plan, through emblazoning with still more conspicuous exploits, their record of stewardship to a Faith whose Author has issued such a ringing call to the rulers of the American continent, and the Center of Whose Covenant has entrusted the American Bahá'í Community with so glorious a mission. Indeed the present stage in the construction of the superstructure of so holy a shrine imperatively demands a concentration of attention and resources commensurate with the high position occupied by this community, with the freedom it enjoys and the material means at its disposal. The signing of two successive contracts, for the masonry of the octagon, the cylinder and the dome of the edifice, necessitated by a sudden worsening of the international situation, which might cut off indefinitely the provision of the same stones used for the erection of the arcade and the parapet of that Sepulcher, and amounting to no less than one hundred and ninety thousand dollars; the subsidiary contracts for the provision of steel and cement for the erection of the wrought iron balustrade and the metal window frames of both the octagon and the cylinder, involving an additional expenditure of no less than twenty thousand dollars, to which must be added the cost of the excavation for and the sinking of the eight piers designed to support the weight of the dome and the immediate construction of the octagon—these call for a stupendous effort on the part of all Bahá'í communities and a self-abnegation unprecedented in Bahá'í history. A drastic reduction of national and local budgets; the allocation of substantial sums by all national assemblies; the participation of individuals through sustained and direct donations to the first international and incomparably holy enterprise synchronizing with the birth of the International Bahá'í Council at the very heart and center of a world-encircling Faith can alone insure the uninterrupted progress of an undertaking which, coupled with the completion of the Mother Temple of the West, cannot fail to produce tremendous repercussions in the Holy Land, in the North American continent and throughout the world. A period of austerity covering the two-year interval separating us from the Centenary celebrations of the Year Nine, prolonging so unexpectedly the austerity period already traversed by the American Bahá'í Community, and now extended to embrace its sister communities throughout the Bahá'í world, is evidently not only essential for the attainment of so transcendent a goal, but also supremely befitting when we recall the nature and dimensions of the holocaust which a hundred years ago crimson-dyed the annals of our Faith, which posterity will recognize as the bloodiest episode of the most tragic period of the Heroic Age of the Bahá'í Dispensation, which involved the martyrdom of that incomparable heroine Ṭáhirih, which was immediately preceded by the imprisonment of Bahá'u'lláh in the subterranean dungeon of Ṭihrán, and which sealed the fate of thousands of men, women and children in circumstances of unspeakable savagery and on a scale unapproached throughout subsequent stages of Bahá'í history.

No Sacrifice Too Great

No sacrifice can be deemed too great, no expenditure of material resources, no degree of renunciation of worldly benefits, comfort and pleasures, can be regarded as excessive when we recall the precious blood that flowed, the many lives that were snuffed out, the wealth of material possessions that was plundered during these most tumultuous and cataclysmic years of the Heroic Age of our Faith.

Nor will the sacrifices willingly and universally accepted by the followers of the Faith in East and West for the sake of so noble a Cause, so transcendent an enterprise, fail to contribute their share towards the upbuilding of the World Administrative Center of that Faith, and the reinforcement of the ties already linking this Center with the recognized authorities of a state under the jurisdiction of which it is now functioning, ties which the newly formed International Bahá'í Council are so assiduously striving to cement.

Already the completion of the construction of the arcade of this majestic Sepulcher and of its ornamental parapet has excited the admiration, stimulated the interest, and enlisted the support, of both the local authorities and of the central government, as evidenced by the series of acts which, ever since the emergence of that state, have proclaimed the good will shown and the recognition extended by the various departments of that state to the multiplying international institutions, endowments, laws and ordinances of a steadily rising Faith.

The recognition of the sacred nature of the twin holy Shrines, situated in the plain of 'Akká and on the slopes of Mount Carmel; the exemption from state and civic taxes, granted to the mansion of Bahjí adjoining the Most Holy Shrine, to the twin houses, that of Bahá'u'lláh in 'Akká, and 'Abdu'l-Bahá in Haifa, to the twin archives, adjoining the Shrine of the Báb and the resting-place of the Greatest Holy Leaf, and the twin pilgrim houses constructed in the neighborhood of that Shrine, and of the residence of 'Abdu'l-Bahá; the delivery of the mansion of Mazra'ih by the authorities of that same state to the Bahá'í Community and its occupation after a lapse of more than fifty years; the setting apart, through government action, of the room occupied by Bahá'u'lláh in the barracks of 'Akká, as a place of pilgrimage; the recognition of the Bahá'í marriage certificate by the District Commissioner of Haifa; the recognition of the Bahá'í holy days, in an official circular published by the Ministry of Education and Culture; the exemption from duty accorded by the Customs Department to all furniture received for Bahá'í holy places as well as for all material imported for the construction of the Báb's Sepulcher, the exemption from taxes similarly extended to all international Bahá'í endowments surrounding the holy tomb on Mount Carmel, stretching from the ridge of the mountain to the Templar colony at its foot, as well as to the holdings in the immediate vicinity of the resting-place of the Greatest Holy Leaf and her kinsmen—all these establish, beyond the shadow of a doubt, the high status enjoyed by the international institutions of a world Faith, in the eyes of this newborn state.

The construction of the mausoleum of the Báb, synchronizing with the birth of that state, and the progress of which has been accompanied by these successive manifestations of the good will and support of the civil authorities will, if steadily maintained, greatly reinforce, and lend a tremendous impetus to this process of recognition which constitutes an historic landmark in the evolution of the World Center of the Faith of Bahá'u'lláh—a process which the newly formed Council, now established at its very heart, is designed to foster, which will gather momentum, with the emergence in the course of time of a properly recognized and independently functioning Bahá'í court, which will attain its consummation in the institution of the Universal House of Justice and the emergence of the auxiliary administrative agencies, revolving around this highest legislative body, and which will reveal the plenitude of its potentialities with the sailing of the Divine Ark as promised in the Tablet of Carmel.

I cannot at this juncture over emphasize the sacredness of that holy dust embosomed in the heart of the Vineyard of God, or overrate the unimaginable potencies of this mighty institution founded sixty years ago, through the operation of the Will of, and the definite selection made by, the Founder of our Faith, on the occasion of His historic visit to that holy mountain, nor can I lay too much stress on the role which this institution, to which the construction of the superstructure of this edifice is bound to lend an unprecedented impetus, is destined to play in the unfoldment of the World Administrative Center of the Faith of Bahá'u'lláh and in the efflorescence of its highest institutions constituting the embryo of its future World Order.

The Center of Nine Concentric Circles

For, just as in the realm of the spirit, the reality of the Báb has been hailed by the Author of the Bahá'í Revelation as "The Point round Whom the realities of the Prophets and Messengers revolve," so, on this visible plane, His sacred remains constitute the heart and center of what may be regarded as nine concentric circles, paralleling thereby, and adding further emphasis to the central position accorded by the Founder of our Faith to One "from Whom God hath caused to proceed the knowledge of all that was and shall be," "the Primal Point from which have been generated all created things."

The outermost circle in this vast system, the visible counterpart of the pivotal position conferred on the Herald of our Faith, is none other than the entire planet. Within the heart of this planet lies the "Most Holy Land," acclaimed by 'Abdu'l-Bahá as "the Nest of the Prophets" and which must be regarded as the center of the world and the Qiblih of the nations. Within this Most Holy Land rises the Mountain of God of immemorial sanctity, the Vineyard of the Lord, the Retreat of Elijah, Whose return the Báb Himself symbolizes. Reposing on the breast of this holy mountain are the extensive properties permanently dedicated to, and constituting the sacred precincts of, the Báb's holy Sepulcher. In the midst of these properties, recognized as the international endowments of the Faith, is situated the most holy court, an enclosure comprising gardens and terraces which at once embellish, and lend a peculiar charm to, these sacred precincts. Embosomed in these lovely and verdant surroundings stands in all its exquisite beauty the mausoleum of the Báb, the shell designed to preserve and adorn the original structure raised by 'Abdu'l-Bahá as the tomb of the Martyr-Herald of our Faith. Within this shell is enshrined that Pearl of Great Price, the holy of holies, those chambers which constitute the tomb itself, and which were constructed by 'Abdu'l-Bahá. Within the heart of this holy of holies is the tabernacle, the vault wherein reposes the most holy casket. Within this vault rests the alabaster sarcophagus in which is deposited that inestimable jewel, the Báb's holy dust. So precious is this dust that the very earth surrounding the edifice enshrining this dust has been extolled by the Center of Bahá'u'lláh's Covenant, in one of His Tablets in which He named the five doors belonging to the six chambers which He originally erected after five of the believers associated with the construction of the Shrine, as being endowed with such potency as to have inspired Him in bestowing these names, whilst the tomb itself housing this dust He acclaimed as the spot round which the Concourse on high circle in adoration.

To participate in the erection of the superstructure of an edifice at once so precious, so holy; consecrated to the memory of so heroic a Soul; whose site no one less than the Founder of our Faith has selected; whose inner chambers were erected by the Center of His Covenant with such infinite care and anguish; embosomed in so sacred a mountain, on the soil of so holy a land; occupying such a unique position; facing on the one hand the silver-white city of 'Akká, the Qiblih of the Bahá'í world; flanked on its right by the hills of Galilee, the home of Jesus Christ, and on its left, by the Cave of Elijah; and backed by the plain of Sharon and, beyond it, Jerusalem and the Aqsá mosque, the third holiest shrine in Islám—to participate in the erection of such an edifice is a privilege offered to this generation at once unique and priceless, a privilege which only posterity will be able to correctly appraise.

THE CHOSEN TRUSTEES OF A DIVINE PLAN

In this supreme, this sacred and international undertaking in which the followers of Bahá'u'lláh, in all the continents of the globe, are summoned to show forth the noblest spirit of self-sacrifice, the members of the American Bahá'í Community must by virtue of the abilities they have already demonstrated and of the primacy conferred upon them as the chosen trustees of a Divine Plan, play a preponderating role, and, together with their brethren residing in the cradle of their Faith, who are linked by such unique ties with its Herald, set an example of self-abnegation worthy to be emulated by their fellow-workers in every land.

Whilst the members of this privileged community, laboring so valiantly in the Western Hemisphere, are widening the range of their manifold activities, and thereby augmenting their responsibilities, in both the Holy Land and the African continent, the original tasks, associated with the prosecution of the Second Seven Year Plan, must, simultaneously with this added and meritorious effort which is being exerted, in memory of the beloved Báb, and for the spiritual emancipation of the downtrodden races of Africa, be carried to a triumphant conclusion. Though the present deficit in their National Fund may, in a sense, register a failure on their part to meet their pressing obligations, and may arouse in their hearts feelings of self-reproach and anxiety, I can confidently assert that the supplementary duties they have discharged, and the material support they have extended, and are now extending, for the conduct of activities, not falling within the original scope of their Plan, not only fully compensate for an apparent shortcoming, but constitute, instead of a stain on their record of service, additional embellishments to the scroll already inscribed with so many exploits for the Cause of Bahá'u'lláh.

Assured that no blot has marred so splendid a record of service; confident of their destiny; reliant on the unfailing guidance of the Founder of their Faith as well as on His sustaining power, let them address themselves, with unrelaxing vigilance and undiminished vigor, to the task of rounding off the several missions undertaken by them in Latin America, and in the North American and European continents.

The extension of the necessary material support and administrative guidance to the forthcoming national assemblies of Central and South America that will enable them to develop along sound lines and without any setback in the course of their unfoldment; the steady consolidation of the victories already won in the ten goal countries of Europe; the maintenance, at its present level and at whatever cost, of the status of the assemblies and groups so laboriously built up; the provision of whatever is required to fully complete the interior of the Temple and beautify the grounds surrounding it, in preparation for its formal inauguration and its use for public worship—these should be regarded as the essential objectives of the American Bahá'í Community during the two-year interval separating us from the Centenary celebrations of the prophetic mission of the Founder of our Faith.

Time is running short. The effort required to discharge the manifold responsibilities now challenging the members of a lion-hearted community is truly colossal. The issues at stake, demanding every ounce of their energy, are incomparably glorious. An ominous international situation emphasizes this challenge and reinforces the urgency of these issues. In the Holy Land, amid the tribes of a dark continent, over the wide expanses stretching from Panama to the extremity of Chile, in the heart of its own homeland, as well as in the new European field, marking the projection of its world mission across the seas, the American Bahá'í Community must deploy its forces, hoist still higher its pennants, and erect still more glorious memorials to the heroism, the constancy and the devotion of its members. 'Abdu'l-Bahá, Whose Plan they are executing in both hemispheres, and to Whose summons they are now responding in the African continent; the Báb, Whose Sepulcher they are helping to erect; above all Bahá'u'lláh, Whose embryonic World Order they are building in the Holy Land and in other continents of the globe, look down upon them from Their retreats of glory, applauding their acts, guiding their footsteps, vouchsafing Their blessings, and laying up, in the storehouses of the Abhá kingdom such treasures as only They can bestow.

May the members of this community prove themselves, as they forge ahead and approach yet another milestone on the broad highway of their mission, worthy of still greater prizes, and fit to launch still mightier enterprises, for the glory of the Name they bear, and in the service of the Faith they profess.

[March 29, 1951]

First American Pioneer to Africa

Rejoice at departure of first pioneer to Africa; urge acceleration of historic process now set in motion. Time is short, tasks ahead manifold, pressing, momentous. Praying ardently for increasing response and befitting discharge of mighty supplementary task shouldered by valorous community.

[October 19, 1951]

Message to 1951 State Conventions

Advise assembled friends to focus attention on vital, pressing, paramount needs of National Fund at this critical juncture. Hour is ripe to recall unnumbered tribulations, sacrifices heroically endured by the dawn-breakers, culminating in Bahá'u'lláh's afflictive imprisonment in Síyáh Chál, Centennial of which is now approaching. Urge deepening realization of sacredness, preeminent importance of twin purposes which individual resolves serve. Appeal for immediate, unanimous, sustained, decisive response, safeguard thereby American Community's share in tribute to memory of Founder of Faith on occasion of forthcoming Jubilee of Birth of glorious Mission. Praying for befitting answer to heartfelt plea.

[November 4, 1951]

The Last and Irretrievable Chance

The brief interval separating the hard-pressed, valiantly struggling, resistlessly expanding American Bahá'í Community from the anticipated consummation of the second, fate-laden collective enterprise launched so auspiciously by its national elected representatives is speedily drawing to a close. The sixteen months that still lie ahead constitute in view of the tasks that still remain to be achieved, and the sacrifices still to be made, a period at once critical and challenging. This memorable period commemorates, if we pause and call to mind the stirring events and bloody episodes linking the Dispensation of the Báb with the dawning Mission of the Founder of our Faith, the centenary of what may be truly regarded as the darkest, the most tragic, the most heroic, period in the annals of a hundred-year-old Revelation. This period, moreover, affords the last and irretrievable chance to a ceaselessly striving, repeatedly victorious community of setting the seal of triumph upon a momentous undertaking, on whose fate hinges the launching of yet another glorious Crusade, the consummation of which will mark the successful conclusion of the initial epoch in the unfoldment of 'Abdu'l-Bahá's Divine Plan—an evolution that must continue to blossom and fructify in the course of successive epochs of the Formative Ages of the Faith, and yield its fairest fruit in the Golden Age that is yet to come.

A Period of Historic Significance

The historic significance of this period cannot indeed be overestimated. For it was a hundred years ago that a Faith, which had already been oppressed by a staggering weight of untold tribulations; which had sustained shattering blows in Mázindarán, Nayríz, Ṭihrán and Zanján, and indeed throughout every province in the land of its birth; which had lost its greatest exponents through the tragic martyrdom of most of the Letters of the Living, and particularly of the valiant Mullá Ḥusayn and of the erudite Vaḥíd and which had been afflicted with the supreme calamity of losing its Divine Founder; was being subjected to still more painful ordeals—ordeals which robbed it of both the heroic Ḥujjat and of the far-famed Ṭáhirih; which caused it to pass through a reign of terror, and to experience a blood-bath of unprecedented severity, which inflicted on it one of the greatest humiliations it has ever suffered through the attempted assassination of the sovereign himself, and which unloosed a veritable deluge of barbarous atrocities in Ṭihrán, Mázindarán, Nayríz and Shíráz before which paled the horrors of the siege of Zanján, and which swept no less a figure than Bahá'u'lláh Himself—the last remaining pillar of a Faith that had been so rudely shaken, so ruthlessly denuded of its chief buttresses—into the subterranean dungeon of Ṭihrán, an imprisonment that was soon followed by His cruel banishment, in the depths of an exceptionally severe winter, from His native land to 'Iráq. To these tribulations He Himself has referred as "afflictions" that "rained" upon Him, whilst the blood shed by His companions and lovers He characterized as the blood which "impregnated" the earth with the "wondrous revelation" of God's "might."

Nor should the momentous character of the unique event, that may be regarded as the climax and consummation of this tragic period, be overlooked or underestimated, inasmuch as its centenary synchronizes with the termination of the sixteen-month interval separating the American Bahá'í Community from the conclusion of its present Plan.

This unique event, the centenary of which is to be befittingly celebrated, not only in the American continent but throughout the Bahá'í
world, and is destined to be regarded as the culmination of the Second
Seven Year Plan, is none other than the "Year Nine," anticipated 2,000
years ago as the "third woe" by St. John the Divine, alluded to by both
Shaykh Aḥmad and Siyyid Káẓim—the twin luminaries that heralded
the advent of the Faith of the Báb—specifically mentioned and extolled by the Herald of the Bahá'í Dispensation in His Writings, and
eulogized by both the Founder of our Faith and the Center of His
Covenant. In that year, the year "after Hin" (68), mentioned by
Shaykh Aḥmad, the year that witnessed the birth of the Mission of the
promised "Qayyúm," specifically referred to by Siyyid Káẓim, the
"requisite number" in the words of Bahá'u'lláh, "of pure, of wholly
consecrated and sanctified souls" had been "most secretly consummated." In that year, as testified by the pen of the Báb, the "realities
of the created things" were "made manifest," "a new creation was born"
and the seed of His Faith revealed its "ultimate perfection." In that
year, as borne witness by 'Abdu'l-Bahá, a hitherto "embryonic Faith"
was born. In that year, while the Blessed Beauty lay in chains and fetters, in that dark and pestilential pit, "the breezes of the All-Glorious,"
as He Himself described it, "were wafted" over Him. There, whilst His
neck was weighted down by the Qará-Guhar, His feet in stocks, breath-
ing the fetid air of the Síyáh-Chál, He dreamed His dream and heard,
"on every side," "exalted words," and His "tongue recited" words that
"no man could bear to hear."

There, as He Himself has recorded, under the impact of this dream,
He experienced the onrushing force of His newly revealed Mission,
that "flowed" even as "a mighty torrent" from His "head" to His
"breast," whereupon "every limb" of His body "would be set afire."
There, in a vision, the "Most Great Spirit," as He Himself has again
testified, appeared to Him, in the guise of a "Maiden" "calling" with "a
most wondrous, a most sweet voice" above His Head, whilst "suspended in the air" before Him and, "pointing with her finger" unto His
head, imparted "tidings which rejoiced" His "soul." There appeared
above the horizon of that dungeon in the city of Ṭihrán, the rim of the
Orb of His Faith, whose dawning light had, nine years previously,
broken upon the city of Shíráz—an Orb which, after suffering an
eclipse of ten years, was destined to burst forth, with its resplendent

rays, upon the city of Baghdád, to mount its zenith in Adrianople, and to set eventually in the prison-fortress of 'Akká.

Such is the year we are steadily approaching. Such is the year with which the fortunes of the Second Seven Year Plan have been linked. As the tribulations, humiliations and trials inflicted on the Cause of God in Persia, a century ago, moved inexorably towards a climax, so must the present austerity period, inaugurated a hundred years later, in the continent of America, to reflect the privations and sacrifices endured so stoically by the dawn-breakers of the Heroic Age of the Faith witness, as it approaches its culmination, a self-abnegation on the part of the champion-builders of the World Order of Bahá'u'lláh, laboring in the present Formative Age of His Faith, which, at its best, can be regarded as but a faint reflection of the self-sacrifice so gloriously evinced by their spiritual forbears.

Objectives of Second Seven Year Plan Largely Attained

The objectives of the Second Seven Year Plan, the concluding phase of which has synchronized with this period of nation-wide austerity, have, it must be recognized, been in the main, attained. The pillars which must needs add their strength in supporting the future House of Justice have, according to the schedule laid down, been successively erected in the Dominion of Canada and in Latin America. The European Teaching Campaign—the second outstanding enterprise launched, beyond the confines of the North American continent, in pursuance of the Mandate, issued by 'Abdu'l-Bahá to Bahá'u'lláh's valiant "Apostles"—has not only achieved its original aims, but exceeded all expectations through the formation of a local spiritual assembly in the capital city of each of the ten goal countries included within its scope. The interior ornamentation of the Mother Temple of the West has, before its appointed time, been completed. Other tasks, no less vital, still remain to be carried, in the course of a fast shrinking period, to a successful conclusion. The landscaping of the area surrounding a structure whose foundations and exterior and interior ornamentation have demanded, for so many years, so much effort and such constant sacrifice, must, under no circumstances, and while there is yet time, be neglected, lest failure to achieve this final task mar the beauty of the approaches of a national shrine which provide so suitable a setting for an edifice at once so sacred and noble. The responsibilities solemnly undertaken to consolidate and multiply the administrative institutions throughout all the states of the Union—a task that has of late been allowed to fall into abeyance, and has been eclipsed by the spectacular success attending the shining exploits of the American Bahá'í Community in foreign fields—must be speedily and seriously reconsidered, for upon the constant broadening and the steady reinforcement of this internal administrative structure, which provides the essential base for future operations in all the continents of the globe, must depend the vigor, the rapidity and the soundness of the future crusades which must needs be launched in the service, and for the glory of the Faith of Bahá'u'lláh, and in obedience to the stirring summons issued by the Center of His Covenant in some of His most weighty Tablets. Above all, the accumulating deficit which has lately again thrown its somber shadow on an otherwise resplendent record of service, must, through a renewed display of self-abnegation, which, though not commensurate with the sacrifice of so many souls immolated on the altar of the Faith of Bahá'u'lláh, may at least faintly reflect its poignant heroism, be obliterated, once and for all, from the record of a splendid stewardship to His Faith.

There can be no doubt—and I am the first to proudly acknowledge it—that, ever since the launching of the Second Seven Year Plan, and in consequence of unexpected developments both in the Holy Land and elsewhere, the American Bahá'í Community, ever ready to bear the brunt of responsibility, under the stress of unforeseen circumstances, has considerably widened the scope of its original undertakings and augmented the weight shouldered by its stalwart members. At the World Center of the Faith, in response to the urgent call for action, necessitated by the imperative needs of the rising Sepulcher of the Báb, the formation of the Bahá'í International Council, and the establishment of the State of Israel, as well as in the continent of Africa, where the appointed, the chief trustees of a divinely conceived, world-encompassing Plan could not well remain unmoved by the sight of the first attempts being made to introduce systematically the Faith of Bahá'u'lláh and to implant its banner amongst its tribes and races, the American Bahá'í Community have assumed responsibilities well exceeding the original duties they had undertaken to discharge. This twofold opportunity that providentially presented itself to them, to contribute to the rise and consolidation of the World Center of their Faith, and to the spiritual re-awakening of a long-neglected continent, must, however, be exploited to the fullest extent, if the early completion of the most sacred edifice, next to the Qiblih of the Bahá'í world, is to be assured, and if the executors of 'Abdu'l-Bahá's Plan are to retain untarnished the primacy conferred upon them by its Author.

That primacy will be demonstrated and re-emphasized as the representatives of this privileged community take their place, and assume their functions, at each of the four Intercontinental Bahá'í Teaching Conferences which are to be convened in the course of, and which must signalize, the world-wide celebrations of the Centenary of the Year Nine. Playing a preponderating role, as the custodians of a Divine Plan, in the global crusade which all the Bahá'í national spiritual assemblies, without exception, must, in various degrees and combinations, launch on the morrow of the forthcoming Centenary, and during the entire course of the ten-year interval separating them from the Most Great Jubilee, they must, upon the consummation of their present Plan, deliberate, together with their ally the Canadian National Assembly, and their associates, the newly formed National Spiritual Assemblies of Central and South America, on the occasion of the convocation of the approaching All-American Teaching Conference, on ways and means whereby they can best contribute to the establishment of the Faith, not only throughout the Americas and their neighboring islands, but in the chief sovereign states and dependencies of the remaining continents of the globe.

SCOPE OF THIRD SEVEN YEAR PLAN WIDENED

For unlike the First and Second Seven Year Plans, inaugurated by the American Bahá'í Community, the scope of the Third Seven Year Plan, the termination of which will mark the conclusion of the first epoch in the evolution of the Master Plan designed by 'Abdu'l-Bahá, will embrace all the continents of the earth, and will bring the central body directing these widely ramified operations into direct contact with all the national assemblies of the Bahá'í world, which, in varying degrees, will have to contribute their share to the world establishment of the Cause of Bahá'u'lláh, as prophesied by 'Abdu'l-Bahá and envisioned by Daniel—a consummation that, God willing, will be befittingly celebrated on the occasion of the Most Great Jubilee commemorating the hundredth anniversary of the formal assumption by Bahá'u'lláh of His Prophetic Office.

The vision now disclosed to the eyes of this community is indeed enthralling. The tasks which, if that vision is to be fulfilled, must be valiantly shouldered by its members are staggering. The time during which so herculean a task is to be performed is alarmingly brief. The period during which so gigantic an operation must be set in motion, prosecuted and consummated, coincides with the critical, and perhaps the darkest and most tragic, stage in human affairs. The opportunities presenting themselves to them are now close at hand. The invisible battalions of the Concourse on High are mustered, in serried ranks, ready to rush their reinforcements to the aid of the vanguard of Bahá'u'lláh's crusaders in the hour of their greatest need, and in anticipation of that Most Great, that Wondrous Jubilee in the joyfulness of which both heaven and earth will partake. 'Abdu'l-Bahá, the Founder of this community and the Author of the Plan which constitutes its birthright, to Whose last wishes its members so marvelously responded; the Báb, the Centenary of Whose Revelation this same community so magnificently celebrated, and to the building of whose Sepulcher it has given so fervent a support; Bahá'u'lláh Himself, to the glory of Whose Name so stately an edifice it has raised, will amply bless and repay its members if they but persevere on the long road they have so steadfastly trodden, and pursue, with undimmed vision, with unrelaxing resolve and unshakable faith, their onward march towards their chosen goal.

That this community, so young in years, yet withal so rich in exploits, may, in the months immediately ahead, as well as in the years immediately following this coming Jubilee, maintain, untarnished and unimpaired, its record of service to our beloved Faith, that it may further embellish, through still nobler feats, its annals, is the dearest wish of my heart, and the object of my constant supplications at the Holy Threshold.

[November 23, 1951]

Funds for International Center

Deeply touched by reconsecration and readiness to sacrifice. Praying for fulfilment of your hopes. Advise allocate substantial portion of budget to meet continual needs arising at International Center of Faith.

[May 3, 1952]

Forty-Fifth Annual Convention: U.S. Tasks in World Crusade

My soul is uplifted in joy and thanksgiving at the triumphant conclusion of the Second Seven Year Plan immortalized by the brilliant victories simultaneously won by the vanguard of the hosts of Bahá'u'lláh in Latin America, in Europe and in Africa—victories befittingly crowned through the consummation of a fifty year old enterprise, the completion of the first Mashriqu'l-Adhkár of the western world. The signal success that has attended the second collective enterprise undertaken in the course of American Bahá'í history climaxes a term of stewardship to the Faith of Bahá'u'lláh, of almost three score years' duration—a period which has enriched the annals of the concluding epoch of the Heroic, and shed luster on the first thirty years of the Formative Age of the Bahá'í Dispensation. So fecund a period has been marked by teaching activities unexcelled throughout the western world and has been distinguished by administrative exploits unparalleled in the annals of any Bahá'í national community whether in the East or in the West. I am impelled, on the occasion of the anniversary of the Most Great Festival, coinciding with a triple celebration—the dedication of the Mother Temple of the West, the launching of a World Spiritual Crusade and the commemoration of the Birth of Bahá'u'lláh's Mission—to pay warmest tribute to the preeminent share which the American Bahá'í Community has had in the course of over half a century in proclaiming His Revelation, in shielding His Cause, in championing His Covenant, in erecting the administrative machinery of His embryonic World Order, in expounding His teachings, in translating and disseminating His Holy Word, in dispatching the messengers of His Glad Tidings, in awakening royalty to His Call, in succoring His oppressed followers, in routing His enemies, in upholding His Law, in asserting the independence of His Faith, in multiplying the financial resources of its nascent institutions and, last but not least, in rearing its greatest House of Worship—the first Mashriqu'l-Adhkár of the western world.

The hour is now ripe for this greatly gifted, richly blessed community to arise and reaffirm, through the launching of yet another enterprise, its primacy, enhance its spiritual heritage, plumb greater depths of consecration and capture loftier heights in the course of its strenuous and ceaseless labors for the exaltation of God's Cause.

The Ten Year Plan, constituting the third and final stage of the initial epoch in the evolution of 'Abdu'l-Bahá's Master Plan, which, God willing, will raise to greater heights the fame of the stalwart American Bahá'í Community, and seat it upon "the throne of an everlasting dominion," envisaged by the Author of the Tablets of this same Plan, involves:

First, the opening of the following virgin territories, eleven in Africa: Cape Verde Islands, Canary Islands, French Somaliland, French Togoland, Mauritius, Northern Territories Protectorate, Portuguese Guinea, Reunion Island, Spanish Guinea, St. Helena and St. Thomas Island; eight in Asia: Caroline Islands, Dutch New Guinea, Hainan Island, Kazakhstan, Macao Island, Sakhalin Island, Tibet and Tonga Islands; six in Europe: Andorra, Azores, Balearic Islands, Lofoten Islands, Spitzbergen and Ukraine; and four in America: Aleutian Islands, Falkland Islands, Key West and Kodiak Island.

Second, the consolidation of the Faith in the following territories, six in Asia: China, Formosa, Japan, Korea, Manchuria, Philippine Islands; two in Africa: Liberia and South Africa; twelve in Europe: the ten goal countries, Finland and France; three in America: the Hawaiian Islands, Alaska and Puerto Rico.

Third, the extension of assistance to the National Spiritual Assemblies of the Bahá'ís of Central and South America, as well as to the National Spiritual Assembly of the Bahá'ís of Italy and Switzerland in forming twenty national spiritual assemblies in the republics of Latin America and two in Europe, namely in Italy and Switzerland; the extension of assistance for the establishment of a national Ḥaẓíratu'l-Quds in the capital of each of the aforementioned countries as well as of national Bahá'í endowments in these same countries.

Fourth, the establishment of ten national spiritual assemblies in the following European countries: Sweden, Norway, Denmark, Belgium, Holland, Luxembourg, Spain, Portugal, France and Finland.

Fifth, the establishment of a national spiritual assembly in Japan and one in the South Pacific Islands.

Sixth, the establishment of the National Spiritual Assembly of the Bahá'ís of Alaska.

Seventh, the establishment of the National Spiritual Assembly of the Bahá'ís of South and West Africa.

Eighth, the incorporation of each of the fourteen above-mentioned national spiritual assemblies.

Ninth, the establishment of national Bahá'í endowments by these same national spiritual assemblies.

Tenth, the establishment of a national Ḥaẓíratu'l-Quds in the capital city of each of the eleven of the aforementioned countries, as well as one in Anchorage, one in Suva, and one in Johannesburg.

Eleventh, the erection of the first dependency of the first Mashriqu'l-Adhkár of the western world.

Twelfth, the extension of assistance for the purchase of land for four future Temples, two in Europe: in Stockholm and Rome; one in Central America, in Panama City; and one in Africa, in Johannesburg.

Thirteenth, the completion of the landscaping of the grounds of the Mashriqu'l-Adhkár in Wilmette.

Fourteenth, the raising to one hundred of the number of incorporated local assemblies within the American Union.

Fifteenth, the raising to three hundred of the number of local spiritual assemblies in that same country.

Sixteenth, the incorporation of spiritual assemblies in the leading cities of Sweden, Norway, Denmark, Belgium, Holland, Luxembourg, Spain and Portugal, as well as of the Spiritual Assemblies of Paris, of Helsingfors, of Tokyo, of Suva and of Johannesburg.

Seventeenth, the quadrupling of the number of local spiritual assemblies and the trebling of the number of localities in the aforementioned countries.

Eighteenth, the translation of Bahá'í literature into ten languages in Europe (Basque, Estonian, Flemish, Lapp, Maltese, Piedmontese, Romani, Romansch, Yiddish and Ziryen; ten in America: Aguaruna, Arawak, Blackfoot, Cherokee, Iroquois, Lengua, Mataco, Maya, Mexican and Yahgan.

Nineteenth, the conversion to the Faith of members of the leading Indian tribes.

Twentieth, the conversion to the Faith of representatives of the Basque and Gypsy races.

Twenty-first, the establishment of summer schools in each of the Scandinavian and Benelux countries, as well as those of the Iberian Peninsula.

Twenty-second, the proclamation of the Faith through the press and radio throughout the United States of America.

Twenty-third, the establishment of a Bahá'í Publishing Trust in Wilmette, Illinois.

Twenty-fourth, the formation of an Asian teaching committee designed to stimulate and coordinate the teaching activities initiated by the Plan.

May this community—the spiritual descendants of the dawn-breakers of the Heroic Age of the Bahá'í Faith, the chief repository of the immortal Tablets of 'Abdu'l-Bahá's Divine Plan, the foremost executors of the Mandate issued by the Center of Bahá'u'lláh's Covenant, the champion-builders of a divinely conceived Administrative Order, the standard-bearers of the all-conquering army of the Lord of Hosts, the torchbearers of a future divinely inspired world civilization—arise, in the course of the momentous decade separating the Great from the Most Great Jubilee to secure, as befits its rank, the lion's share in the prosecution of a global crusade designed to diffuse the light of God's revelation over the surface of the entire planet.

[April 29, 1953]

Intending Pioneers Urged to Scatter

Strongly urge intending pioneers to scatter as widely as possible, settle even territories, islands not specifically assigned to United States. Prompt opening of virgin territories is highly meritorious, extremely urgent, vital prerequisite to insure triumphant conclusion of opening phase of Global Crusade, prerogative of chief executors of 'Abdu'l-Bahá's Plan. May enrolled pioneers arise and confirm primacy of American Bahá'í Community playing preponderating role in initial stage of spiritual conquest of unopened territories and islands of the planet.

[May 13, 1953]

A Turning Point in American Bahá'í History

My soul is thrilled and my heart is filled with gratitude as I contemplate—looking back upon six decades of eventful American Bahá'í history—the chain of magnificent achievements which, from the dawn of the Faith of Bahá'u'lláh in the West until the present day, have signalized the birth, marked the rise and distinguished the unfoldment of the glorious mission of the American Bahá'í Community. Of all Bahá'í communities in both the Eastern and Western Hemispheres, with the sole exception of its venerable sister community in Bahá'u'lláh's native land, it alone may well claim to have released forces, and set in motion events, which stand unparalleled in the annals of the Faith; while in the course of the last fifty years, comprising the concluding years of the Heroic and the opening epochs of the Formative Age of the Bahá'í Dispensation, it can confidently boast of a record of stewardship which, for its scope, effectiveness and splendor, is unmatched by that of any other community in the entire Bahá'í world.

The first to awaken to the call of the New Day in the western world; the first to spontaneously arise to befittingly erect the Mother Temple of the West; the first to grasp the implications, evolve the pattern and lay the basis of the structure of the Bahá'í Administrative Order in the entire Bahá'í world; the first to openly and systematically proclaim the fundamental principles of the Faith, to adopt effectual measures for its defense, to invite the attention of royalty to its teachings, to devise an adequate machinery for the translation, the publication and the dissemination of its literature and to provide the means for the creation of its subsidiary institutions; the first to champion the cause of the oppressed and to generously contribute to the alleviation of the sufferings of the needy and persecuted among the followers of Bahá'u'lláh; the first to inaugurate collective enterprises for the propagation of His Cause; the first to assert its independence in the West; the first to lay an unassailable foundation for the erection of auxiliary institutions designed to multiply its financial resources; and, more recently, the first to achieve, as befits its primacy, the initial task devolving upon it in pursuance of the newly launched World Spiritual

Crusade, this community has abundantly merited, by the quality of its deeds and the magnitude of its exploits, the distinctive titles of the cradle of the World Order of Bahá'u'lláh, of the vanguard of His world-conquering host, of the standard-bearers of the oneness of mankind, of the chief trustees of the Plan devised by the Center of the Covenant and of the torch-bearers of an as yet unborn world civilization.

RECENT SERVICES DESERVING MENTION

The services rendered by this same community in recent years, in its capacity as the chief executors of 'Abdu'l-Bahá's Divine Plan, in the course of the second stage of the initial epoch in its evolution, are of such importance and significance as to deserve particular mention at this time. In the North American continent, throughout the republics of Latin America, in the ten goal countries of Europe, on the shores and in the heart of the African continent, the members of this community have, in conformity with the provisions of the Second Seven Year Plan, performed feats of such noble and enduring heroism as to enhance immensely their prestige, demonstrate unmistakably the caliber of their faith and qualify them to assume a preponderating share in the prosecution of the Ten Year Plan whose operations are to extend over the entire surface of the globe.

In the multiplication and consolidation of Bahá'í administrative institutions and their auxiliary agencies throughout Central America, the Antilles and every South American republic—a task supplementing the initial enterprise undertaken, in pursuance of the first Seven Year Plan, in connection with the introduction of the Faith into the republics of Latin America; in the even more rapid development of nascent institutions of the Faith in Scandinavia, in the Benelux countries, in Switzerland, in the Italian and Iberian Peninsulas; in the laying of the administrative basis of the World Order of Bahá'u'lláh in the capital and in some of the major cities of each of the ten European sovereign states included within the scope of the Plan; in the convocation of a series of historic teaching conferences in the north and in the heart of the European continent—heralding the convocation of the recently held, epoch-making Intercontinental Teaching Conferences; in the translation, the publication and dissemination of Bahá'í literature in various European languages; in the still more dramatic evolution of the Faith in the African continent, culminating in the convocation of the first Intercontinental Teaching Conference of the Holy Year in the heart of Africa; in the tremendous sacrifices spontaneously and repeatedly made to broaden and reinforce the foundations of the Faith in the North American continent, to sustain the campaigns undertaken in Latin America, Europe and Africa, and to meet the many demands of the Bahá'í Temple, rapidly nearing completion in Wilmette; in the successive emergence of three national spiritual assemblies in the Western Hemisphere—an outstanding contribution to the evolution and consolidation of the structure of the world Administrative Order of the Faith; in the completion of the interior ornamentation of the first Mashriqu'l-Adhkár of the West, the provision of its accessories and the initiation of the landscaping of its grounds; in the support extended to the development of the institutions of the World Center of the Faith; in the role played by its representatives, whether as Hands of the Cause or members of the International Bahá'í Council; in the financial aid unhesitatingly given to hasten the construction, and insure the completion, of the superstructure of the Báb's Sepulcher on Mt. Carmel—above all, in the share its national elected representatives have assumed in providing the means for the convocation of the second Intercontinental Teaching Conference of the Holy Year; in commemorating worthily the dedication to public worship of the Mother Temple of the West, on the occasion of its Jubilee; in befittingly inaugurating the launching of the World Spiritual Crusade, and in celebrating the climax of the Holy Year marking the centenary of the birth of Bahá'u'lláh's Mission—in all these the American Bahá'í Community has fully deserved the praise and gratitude of posterity, has merited the applause of the Concourse on High and earned a full measure of the divine blessings and of the celestial sustenance of which it will stand in such great need in the course of the prosecution of still mightier and more glorious enterprises in the days to come.

ADDED RESPONSIBILITIES IN PROPAGATING THE DIVINE PLAN

The stage is now set, and the hour propitious, for a deployment of forces, and for the revelation of the indomitable spirit animating this community, on a scale and to a degree unprecedented in the entire course of American Bahá'í history. To the Antilles and the seventeen republics of Central and of South America—the scene of the initial exploits of a community inaugurating the opening phase of its world-girding mission—to the ten sovereign states of Europe which, at a subsequent stage in the unfoldment of that mission, the members of this community enthusiastically and determinedly arose to open up and conquer; to the African territories which, in addition to their allocated task under the Second Seven Year Plan, they spontaneously endeavored to win to the all-conquering Cause of Bahá'u'lláh—to these numerous islands and archipelagos, bordering the American, the European and African continents; dependencies extensive, well-nigh inaccessible, and remote from the base of their operations throughout the Asiatic continent; lastly, the South Pacific area, the home of the one remaining race not as yet adequately represented in the Bahá'í world community, occupying spiritually so strategic a position owing to its proximity to the Bahá'í communities already firmly entrenched in South America, in the Indian subcontinent and in Australasia, at once challenging the resources of no less than eight national spiritual assemblies, and the theater destined to witness the noblest and the most resounding victories which the chosen executors of 'Abdu'l-Bahá's Divine Plan have been called upon to win in the service of the Cause of God—all these have now, in accordance with the requirements of an irresistibly unfolding Plan, been added, completing thereby the full circle of the world-wide obligations devolving upon a community invested with spiritual primacy by the Author of the immortal Tablets constituting the Charter of the Master Plan of the appointed Center of Bahá'u'lláh's Covenant.

"The moment this Divine Message," He Who penned these Tablets and conferred this primacy has most significantly affirmed, "is propagated through the continents of Europe, of Asia, of Africa and of Australasia, and as far as the islands of the Pacific, this community will find itself securely established upon the throne of an everlasting dominion." Then, and only then, will, as He Himself has so remarkably prophesied, "the whole earth" "resound with the praises of its majesty and greatness."

Now, indeed, is the time, after the lapse of two score years; following the triumphant conclusion of two successive historic Plans, marking the opening stages of the first epoch in the unfoldment of that same Master Plan; on the morrow of the brilliant celebrations climaxing the world-wide festivities of a memorable Holy Year; and while a triumphant community, in the first flush of enthusiasm, has just garnered the first fruits of its campaigns in four continents of the globe and is laden with its freshly won trophies, for this community to bestir itself, and, assuming its rightful preponderating share in the conduct of a newly launched World Spiritual Crusade, to demonstrate, through a supreme and sustained effort embracing the entire surface of the planet, its ability to safeguard that primacy, to enrich immeasurably the record of its stewardship and to bring to a majestic conclusion the opening epoch in the evolution of a Plan destined to reveal the full measure of its potentialities, not only throughout the successive epochs of the Formative Age of the Faith, but in the course of the vast reaches of time stretching into the Golden, the last Age of the Bahá'í Dispensation.

A LASTING INFLUENCE ON AMERICAN COMMUNITY AND NATION

This decade-long global Crusade must mark a veritable turning point in American Bahá'í history. It must prove itself to be, as it develops, a force so pervasive and revolutionary in its character as to leave a lasting imprint not only on the destinies of the American Bahá'í Community but on the fortunes of the American nation as well. It must, even as a baptismal fire, so purge its members from self as to enable them to scale heights never as yet attained. It must, in its initial stages, witness a dispersal, combined with a consecration, reminiscent of the dawn of the Heroic Age in Bahá'u'lláh's native land. It must, as it gathers momentum, awaken the select and gather the spiritually hungry amongst the peoples of the world, as well as create an awareness of the Faith not only among the political leaders of present-day society but also among the thoughtful, the erudite in other spheres of human activity. It must, as it approaches its climax, carry the torch of the Faith to regions so remote, so backward, so inhospitable that neither the light of Christianity or Islám has, after the revolution of centuries, as yet penetrated. It must, as it approaches its conclusion, pave the way for the laying, on an unassailable foundation, of the structural basis of an Administrative Order whose fabric must, in the course of successive crusades, be laboriously erected throughout the entire globe and which must assemble beneath its sheltering shadow peoples of every race, tongue, creed, color and nation.

Seconded by the neighboring fully fledged Canadian Bahá'í Community flourishing beyond the northern frontier of its homeland; supported by the newly emerged Latin American communities established in the Antilles and in each of the central and southern republics of the Western Hemisphere; ably aided by its sister community vigorously functioning in the heart of a far-flung empire, and destined to lend its inestimable assistance in the spiritual conquest of the numerous and widely scattered dependencies of the British Crown; reinforced by the oldest and youngest national Bahá'í communities on the European mainland which are to play a prominent part in the eastern and southern regions, and across the frontiers of Europe, along the shores and in the islands of the Mediterranean; assisted by its venerable sister community in the cradle of the Faith and by the second oldest national community in the Bahá'í world actively engaged in the propagation of the Faith in the Asiatic continent; confident of the help of its Egyptian and Indian sister communities, whose destiny is closely linked with the African continent and southeast Asia respectively, and, lastly, assured of the unfailing cooperation of yet another national community in the Antipodes which, owing to its geographical position, is bound to assume a notable share in the introduction of the Faith in the islands of the South Pacific Ocean, the American Bahá'í Community must, as befits its rank as the chief executor of the Divine Plan, play a dominant and decisive role in the direction and control of the manifold operations involved in the prosecution of the North American, the Latin American, the European, the African, the Asian and the South Pacific campaigns of this World Crusade, and insure, by every means at its disposal and in conjunction with its junior partners, its ultimate and total success.

Within its own sphere, extending to every continent of the globe, embracing no less than twenty-nine virgin territories and islands, the members of this stalwart and preeminent community are called upon, among other things and within the relatively brief span of a single decade, to create nuclei, around which will crystallize future assemblies, in no less than eleven territories and islands of Africa, eight of Asia, six of Europe, four of America; to inaugurate the establishment of the future dependencies of the Mother Temple of the West, and to terminate the landscaping of its grounds; to consolidate and broaden the basis of the Administrative Order already laid in twenty-three territories and islands distributed in four continents of the globe and situated in the Atlantic and Pacific Oceans; to assist in the erection of no less than thirty-six pillars, twenty in Latin America, twelve in Europe, two in Asia, one in the North American continent and one in Africa, designed to help in sustaining the weight of the crowning unit of the Bahá'í Administrative Order, and in the establishment of national Bahá'í headquarters, of national endowments, and of national incorporations in all of these continents; to lend its aid for the acquisition of land in anticipation of the erection of four Temples, two in Europe, one in Africa and one in Central America; to lend an impetus to the progress of the Faith in its homeland through raising to three hundred the number of local spiritual assemblies and to one hundred the number of incorporated assemblies, as well as through the founding of a Bahá'í Publishing Trust and the proclamation of the Faith through the press and radio; to enroll in the ranks of the followers of Bahá'u'lláh members of the Indian, of the Basque and Gypsy races; to assume responsibility for the translation and publication of Bahá'í literature in twenty languages, ten in the Americas and ten in Europe; and to contribute to the consolidation of the Faith in eight of the European goal countries through the establishment of local incorporations, as well as through the quadrupling of the number of local assemblies and the trebling of the number of local Bahá'í centers in each one of them.

While this colossal task, which in its magnitude and potentialities transcends any previous collective enterprise launched in the course of American Bahá'í history, is being energetically carried out, it should be constantly borne in mind—and this applies to all communities without exception participating in this World Crusade—that the twofold task of extension and consolidation must be supplemented by continuous and strenuous efforts to increase speedily not only the number of the avowed followers of the Faith in both the virgin and opened territories and islands included within the scope of the Ten Year Plan, but also to swell the ranks of its active supporters who will consecrate their time, resources and energy to the effectual spread of its teachings and the multiplication and consolidation of its administrative institutions.

The movement of pioneers, the opening of virgin territories, the initiation of Houses of Worship and of administrative headquarters, the incorporation of local and national elective bodies, the multiplication of assemblies, groups and isolated centers, the increase in the number of races represented in the world Bahá'í fellowship, the translation, publication and dissemination of Bahá'í literature, the consolidation of administrative agencies and the creation of auxiliary bodies designed to support them, however valuable, essential and meritorious, will in the long run amount to little and fail to achieve their supreme purpose if not supplemented by the equally vital task—which is one that primarily concerns continually and challenges each single individual believer whatever his rank, capacity or origin—of winning to the Faith fresh recruits to the slowly yet steadily advancing army of the Lord of Hosts, whose reinforcing strength is so essential to the safeguarding of the victories which the band of heroic Bahá'í conquerors are winning in the course of their several campaigns in all the continents of the globe.

Such a steady flow of reinforcements is absolutely vital and is of extreme urgency, for nothing short of the vitalizing influx of new blood that will reanimate the world Bahá'í community can safeguard the prizes which, at so great a sacrifice involving the expenditure of so much time, effort and treasure, are now being won in virgin territories by Bahá'u'lláh's valiant Knights, whose privilege is to constitute the spearhead of the onrushing battalions which, in diverse theaters and in circumstances often adverse and extremely challenging, are vying with each other for the spiritual conquest of the unsurrendered territories and islands on the surface of the globe.

This flow, moreover, will presage and hasten the advent of the day which, as prophesied by 'Abdu'l-Bahá, will witness the entry by troops of peoples of divers nations and races into the Bahá'í world—a day which, viewed in its proper perspective, will be the prelude to that long-awaited hour when a mass conversion on the part of these same nations and races, and as a direct result of a chain of events, momentous and possibly catastrophic in nature, and which cannot as yet be even dimly visualized, will suddenly revolutionize the fortunes of the Faith, de-range the equilibrium of the world, and reinforce a thousandfold the numerical strength as well as the material power and the spiritual authority of the Faith of Bahá'u'lláh.

MOST VITAL OBJECTIVE IN THE CRUSADE'S OPENING YEAR

Of all the objectives enumerated in my message to the representatives of this community, assembled on the occasion of the celebration of the climax of the Holy Year, of the convocation of the second Intercontinental Teaching Conference, of the inauguration of the Mother Temple of the West and of the launching of the World Spiritual Crusade, the most vital, urgent and meritorious, in this the opening year of the initial phase of this world-embracing enterprise, is, without doubt, the settlement of pioneers in all the virgin territories and islands assigned to this community in all the continents of the globe, with the exception of the few which, owing to present political obstacles, cannot as yet be opened to the Faith of Bahá'u'lláh. This process already so auspiciously inaugurated, which, in the course of the first eight months of the Holy Year has gathered such splendid momentum, and which bids fair to astonish, stimulate and inspire the entire Bahá'í world, must, during the concluding months of this same year and the one succeding it, be so accelerated as to insure the attainment of this paramount objective before the lapse of two years from the official launching of this World Crusade.

While this goal is being vigorously pursued, close attention must be directed to the preliminary measures for the establishment of the first dependency of the Mother Temple of the West, as well as to the completion of the landscaping of its grounds, a double task that will, on the one hand, mark the termination of the fifty-year-old process of the construction of the central Bahá'í House of Worship, and proclaim, on the other, the commencement of another designed to culminate in the establishment in its plenitude of the institution of the Mashriqu'l-Adhkár as conceived by Bahá'u'lláh and envisaged by 'Abdu'l-Bahá. Moreover, immediate consideration should be given to two other issues of prime importance, namely the purchase of land, which need not exceed for the present one acre, in anticipation of the construction of the first Mashriqu'l-Adhkár of South Africa, and the prompt translation of a suitable Bahá'í pamphlet into the American and European languages allocated to your assembly, and its publication and wide dissemination among the peoples and tribes for whom it has been primarily designed.

The followers of the Most Great Name, citizens of the great republic of the West; constituting the majority and the oldest followers of His Faith in a continent wherein, in the words of 'Abdu'l-Bahá, "the splendors of His (Bahá'u'lláh's) Light shall be revealed" and "the mysteries of His Faith shall be unveiled," addressed by Him in His

Tablets of the Divine Plan as the "Apostles" of His Father; the recipients of the overwhelming majority of these same Tablets constituting the Charter of that Plan; conquerors of most of the territories, whether sovereign states or dependencies, already included within the pale of the Faith; the champion-builders of a world administrative system which posterity will regard as the harbinger of the World Order of Bahá'u'lláh, must, if they wish to retain their primacy and enrich their heritage, insure that, ere the opening of the second phase of this World Crusade, the names of the first American Bahá'í conquerors to settle in virgin territories and islands will, as befits their primacy, be inscribed on the Scroll of Honor, now in process of preparation, and designed to be permanently deposited at the entrance door of the Inner Sanctuary of Bahá'u'lláh's Most Holy Tomb, that the limited area of land required for the erection of four future Bahá'í Temples, in Rome, Stockholm, Panama City and Johannesburg, will be bought, that the landscaping of the grounds of the Temple in Wilmette will be completed, and that the translation and the publication of the aforementioned pamphlet in the specified languages will be accomplished.

The two years that lie ahead, three months of which have already elapsed, will swiftly and imperceptibly draw to a close. Tasks even more onerous, equally weighty and requiring in a still greater measure the expenditure of effort and substance, lie ahead, which will brook no delay, which will carry the Faith to still higher levels of achievement and renown, which will enlarge, through the forging of fresh instruments, the framework of a steadily rising world Administrative Order, and which will eventually, if worthily discharged, seal the triumph of the most prodigious, the most sublime, the most sacred collective enterprise launched by the adherents of the Cause of God in both hemispheres since the early days of the Heroic Age of the Faith—an enterprise which in its vastness, organization and unifying power, has no parallel in the world's spiritual history.

AN APPEAL TO ALL ENGAGED IN THE CRUSADE

To them, and indeed to the entire body of the followers of Bahá'u'lláh, engaged in this global Crusade, I direct my appeal to arise and, in the course of these fast-fleeting years, in every phase of the campaigns that are to be fought in all the continents of the globe, prove their worth as gallant warriors battling for the Cause of Bahá'u'lláh. Indeed, from this very hour until the eve of the Most Great Jubilee, each and every one of those enrolled in the Army of Light must seek no rest, must take no thought of self, must sacrifice to the uttermost, must allow nothing whatsoever to deflect him or her from meeting the pressing, the manifold, the paramount needs of this preeminent Crusade.

"Light as the spirit," "pure as air," "blazing as fire," "unrestrained as the wind"—for such is Bahá'u'lláhs own admonition to His loved ones in His Tablets, and directed not to a select few but to the entire congregation of the faithful—let them scatter far and wide, proclaim the glory of God's Revelation in this Day, quicken the souls of men and ignite in their hearts the love of the One Who alone is their omnipotent and divinely appointed Redeemer.

Bracing the fearful cold of the Arctic regions and the enervating heat of the torrid zone; heedless of the hazards, the loneliness and the austerity of the deserts, the far-away islands and mountains wherein they will be called upon to dwell; undeterred by the clamor which the exponents of religious orthodoxy are sure to raise, or by the restrictive measures which political leaders may impose; undismayed by the smallness of their numbers and the multitude of their potential adversaries; armed with the efficacious weapons their own hands have slowly and laboriously forged in anticipation of this glorious and inevitable encounter with the organized forces of superstition, of corruption and of unbelief; placing their whole trust in the matchless potency of Bahá'u'lláh's teachings, in the all-conquering power of His might and the infallibility of His glorious and oft-repeated promises, let them press forward, each according to his strength and resources, into the vast arena now lying before them, and which, God willing, will witness, in the years immediately lying ahead, such exhibitions of prowess and of heroic self-sacrifice as may well recall the superb feats achieved by that immortal band of God-intoxicated heroes who have so immeasurably enriched the annals of the Christian, the Islamic and Bábi Dispensations.

On the members of the American Bahá'í Community, the envied custodians of a Divine Plan, the principal builders and defenders of a mighty Order and the recognized champions of an unspeakably glorious and precious Faith, a peculiar and inescapable responsibility must necessarily rest. Through their courage, their self-abnegation, their fortitude and their perseverance; through the range and quality of their achievements, the depth of their consecration, their initiative and resourcefulness, their organizing ability, their readiness and capacity to lend their assistance to less privileged sister communities struggling against heavy odds; through their generous and sustained response to the enormous and ever-increasing financial needs of a world-encompassing, decade-long and admittedly strenuous enterprise, they must, beyond the shadow of a doubt, vindicate their right to the leadership of this World Crusade.

Now is the time for the hope voiced by 'Abdu'l-Bahá that from their homeland "heavenly illumination" may "stream to all the peoples of the world" to be realized. Now is the time for the truth of His remarkable assertion that that same homeland is "equipped and empowered to accomplish that which will adorn the pages of history, to become the envy of the world and be blest in both the East and the West," to be strikingly and unmistakably demonstrated. "Should success crown" their "enterprise," He, moreover, has assured them, "the throne of the Kingdom of God will, in the plenitude of its majesty and glory, be firmly established."

Would to God that this community, boasting already of so superb a record of achievements both at home and overseas, and elevated to such dazzling heights by the hopes cherished and the assurance given by the Center of Bahá'u'lláh's Covenant, may prove itself capable of performing deeds of such distinction, in the course of the opening, as well as the succeeding phases of this World Spiritual Crusade, as will outshine the dedicated acts which have already left their indelible mark on the Apostolic Age of the Faith in the West; will excel the enduring, the historic achievements associated, at a later period, with this community's memorable contribution to the rise and establishment of the world Administrative Order of Bahá'u'lláh; will surpass the magnificent accomplishments which, subsequently, as the result of the operation of the first Seven Year Plan, illuminated the annals of the Faith in both the North American continent and throughout Latin America and will eclipse the even more dramatic exploits which, during the opening years of the second epoch of the Formative Age of the Faith, and in the course of the prosecution of the Second Seven Year Plan, have exerted so lasting an influence on the fortunes of the Faith of Bahá'u'lláh in the

Antilles, throughout the republics of Central America, in each of the ten republics of South America, in no less than ten sovereign states in the continent of Europe, and in various dependencies on the eastern and western shores, as well as in the heart of the African continent.

[July 18, 1953]

Safeguarding American Primacy

Overjoyed by remarkable achievements of American Bahá'í Community, safeguarding primacy, enhancing prestige, setting magnificent example to sister communities East and West. Assure three Assembly members, also Lofoten valiant pioneer of abiding appreciation, fervent loving prayers.

[September 5, 1953]

Temple Site Purchased in Panama

Heartfelt congratulations on acquisition of Temple site; notable achievement of World Crusade.

[Circa May 1954]

Assemblies Must Be Maintained

Information incorrect. Maintenance of all assemblies vital.

[July 23, 1954]

(NOTE: *Reply to National Spiritual Assembly request for advice concerning a statement which the Guardian was alleged to have made to the effect that all Bahá'ís should scatter. Many felt, therefore, that assembly status need not be maintained.*)

American Bahá'ís in the Time of World Peril

The American Bahá'í Community, in this, the opening year of the second phase of the World Spiritual Crusade upon which it has embarked, finds itself standing on the threshold of the seventh decade of its existence. It leaves behind it, as it enters the second decade of the second Bahá'í century, sixty years crowded with events and marked by exploits so stirring and momentous that they stand unsurpassed in the annals of any other national Bahá'í community with the sole exception of its venerable sister community in Bahá'u'lláh's native land.

CHIEF EXECUTOR OF DIVINE PLAN

The first to respond to the call of the New Day in the western world; for many years, in concert with the small band of Canadian believers residing in its immediate neighborhood, the sole champion of the newly proclaimed Covenant of Bahá'u'lláh; foremost in its decisive contribution to the creation of the pattern, the erection of the fabric, the enlargement of the limits, and the consolidation of the institutions of the embryonic World Order, the child of that same Covenant and the harbinger of a still unborn world civilization; singled out by the pen of the Center of that same Covenant for a unique and imperishable bounty as the principal custodian and chief executor of 'Abdu'l-Bahá's Divine Plan; doubly honored in the course of His extensive visit to the shores of its homeland through the distinction conferred by Him on the community's two leading centers, the one as the site where He laid the cornerstone of the holiest House of Worship in the Bahá'í world, and the other the scene of the proclamation of His Father's Covenant; the triumphant prosecutor of two successive historic Plans, boldly initiated by its elected national representatives for the propagation of the Faith it has espoused in the land of its birth, in the Dominion of Canada, in Central and South America and in the continent of Europe and for the erection of its own House of Worship, the Mother Temple of the West; outstanding in its role as the defender of the Faith, as the supporter of its down-trodden, long-persecuted sister communities in both the Asiatic and African continents, and as the formulator of the national Bahá'í constitution, embodying the by-laws regulating the internal affairs of the members of the Bahá'í communities; incomparable throughout the Bahá'í world as the dynamic agent responsible for the opening of the vast majority of the over two hundred sovereign states and chief dependencies of the globe to the Faith of Bahá'u'lláh; surpassing even its over a hundred-year old sister community in the cradle of that Faith in the number and variety of isolated centers, groups and local assemblies it has succeeded in establishing over the face of the Union stretching from the Atlantic to the Pacific seaboards and from Alaska to Mexico; noteworthy in the rapid accumulation and wise expenditure of material resources, often involving a self-abnegation reminiscent of the self-sacrifice of the dawn-breakers of the Apostolic Age of the Faith, for the sole purpose of systematically propagating the Faith it has pledged itself to serve, of enhancing its prestige, of multiplying and perfecting its administrative agencies, of enriching its literature, of erecting its edifices, of launching its manifold enterprises, of succoring the needy among the members of its sister communities, of warding off the dangers confronting it from time to time through the malice of its enemies—the American Bahá'í Community, boasting of such a record of exalted service, can well afford to contemplate the immediate future, with its severe challenge, its complex problems, its hazards, tests and trials, with equanimity and confidence.

For there can be no doubt that the entire community, limited as is its numerical strength and circumscribed as are its meager resources, in comparison with the vastness of the field stretching before it, the prodigious efforts demanded of it, and the complexity of the problems it must resolve, stands at a most critical juncture in its history.

AMERICA PASSING THROUGH CRISIS

Moreover, the country of which it forms a part is passing through a crisis which, in its spiritual, moral, social and political aspects, is of extreme seriousness—a seriousness which to a superficial observer is liable to be dangerously underestimated.

The steady and alarming deterioration in the standard of morality as exemplified by the appalling increase of crime, by political corruption in ever widening and ever higher circles, by the loosening of the sacred ties of marriage, by the inordinate craving for pleasure and diversion, and by the marked and progressive slackening of parental control, is no doubt the most arresting and distressing aspect of the decline that has set in, and can be clearly perceived, in the fortunes of the entire nation.

Parallel with this, and pervading all departments of life—an evil which the nation, and indeed all those within the capitalist system, though to a lesser degree, share with that state and its satellites regarded as the sworn enemies of that system—is the crass materialism, which lays excessive and ever-increasing emphasis on material well-being, forgetful of those things of the spirit on which alone a sure and stable foundation can be laid for human society. It is this same cancerous materialism, born originally in Europe, carried to excess in the North American continent, contaminating the Asiatic peoples and nations, spreading its ominous tentacles to the borders of Africa, and now invading its very heart, which Bahá'u'lláh in unequivocal and emphatic language denounced in His Writings, comparing it to a devouring flame and regarding it as the chief factor in precipitating the dire ordeals and world-shaking crises that must necessarily involve the burning of cities and the spread of terror and consternation in the hearts of men. Indeed a foretaste of the devastation which this consuming fire will wreak upon the world, and with which it will lay waste the cities of the nations participating in this tragic world-engulfing contest, has been afforded by the last World War, marking the second stage in the global havoc which humanity, forgetful of its God and heedless of the clear warnings uttered by His appointed Messenger for this day, must, alas, inevitably experience. It is this same all-pervasive, pernicious materialism against which the voice of the Center of Bahá'u'lláh's Covenant was raised, with pathetic persistence, from platform and pulpit, in His addresses to the heedless multitudes, which, on the morrow of His fateful visit to both Europe and America, found themselves suddenly swept into the vortex of a tempest which in its range and severity was unsurpassed in the world's history.

Collateral with this ominous laxity in morals, and this progressive stress laid on man's material pursuits and well-being, is the darkening of the political horizon, as witnessed by the widening of the gulf separating the protagonists of two antagonistic schools of thought which, however divergent in their ideologies, are to be commonly condemned by the upholders of the standard of the Faith of Bahá'u'lláh for their materialistic philosophies and their neglect of those spiritual values and eternal verities on which alone a stable and flourishing civilization can be ultimately established. The multiplication, the diversity and the increasing destructive power of armaments to which both sides, in this world contest, caught in a whirlpool of fear, suspicion and hatred, are rapidly contributing; the outbreak of two successive bloody conflicts, entangling still further the American nation in the affairs of a distracted world, entailing a considerable loss in blood and treasure, swelling the national budget and progressively depreciating the currency of the state; the confusion, the vacillation, the suspicions besetting the European and Asiatic nations in their attitude to the American nation; the overwhelming accretion of strength to the arch enemy of the system championed by the American Union in consequence of the re-alignment of the powers in the Asiatic continent and particularly in the Far East—these have, moreover, contributed their share, in recent years, to the deterioration of a situation which, if not remedied, is bound to involve the American nation in a catastrophe of undreamed-of dimensions and of untold consequences to the social structure, the standard and conception of the American people and government.

No less serious is the stress and strain imposed on the fabric of American society through the fundamental and persistent neglect, by the governed and governors alike, of the supreme, the inescapable and urgent duty—so repeatedly and graphically represented and stressed by 'Abdu'l-Bahá in His arraignment of the basic weaknesses in the social fabric of the nation—of remedying, while there is yet time, through a revolutionary change in the concept and attitude of the average white American toward his Negro fellow citizen, a situation which, if allowed to drift, will, in the words of 'Abdu'l-Bahá, cause the streets of American cities to run with blood, aggravating thereby the havoc which the fearful weapons of destruction, raining from the air, and amassed by a ruthless, a vigilant, a powerful and inveterate enemy, will wreak upon those same cities.

The American nation, of which the community of the Most Great Name forms as yet a negligible and infinitesimal part, stands, indeed, from whichever angle one observes its immediate fortunes, in grave peril. The woes and tribulations which threaten it are partly avoidable, but mostly inevitable and God-sent, for by reason of them a government and people clinging tenaciously to the obsolescent doctrine of absolute sovereignty and upholding a political system, manifestly at variance with the needs of a world already contracted into a neighborhood and crying out for unity, will find itself purged of its anachronistic conceptions, and prepared to play a preponderating role, as foretold by 'Abdu'l-Bahá, in the hoisting of the standard of the Lesser Peace, in the unification of mankind, and in the establishment of a world federal government on this planet. These same fiery tribulations will not only firmly weld the American nation to its sister nations in both hemispheres, but will through their cleansing effect, purge it thoroughly of the accumulated dross which ingrained racial prejudice, rampant materialism, widespread ungodliness and moral laxity have combined, in the course of successive generations, to produce, and which have prevented her thus far from assuming the role of world spiritual leadership forecast by 'Abdu'l-Bahá's unerring pen—a role which she is bound to fulfill through travail and sorrow.

AMERICAN BAHÁ'ÍS STAND AT CROSSROADS

The American Bahá'í Community, the leaven destined to leaven the whole, cannot hope, at this critical juncture in the fortunes of a struggling, perilously situated, spiritually moribund nation, to either escape the trials with which this nation is confronted, nor claim to be wholly immune from the evils that stain its character.

At so critical a period, at so challenging an hour, the members of a community, invested by 'Abdu'l-Bahá with a primacy which can, through neglect and apathy, be allowed to lose its vital power and driving force, are immersed in a task, and are faced with responsibilities, which a World Spiritual Crusade, the third and greatest collective enterprise embarked upon in American Bahá'í history, has thrust upon them before the eyes of their admiring and expectant sister communities throughout the world. They now stand at the crossroads, unable to relax for a moment, or hesitate as to which road they should tread, or to allow any decline in the high standard they have, for no less than six decades, undeviatingly upheld. Nay, if this primacy is to be safeguarded and enhanced, a consecration, not only on the part of a chosen few, to every single objective of the Ten-Year Plan to which they are now pledged, and a pouring out of substance, not only by those of limited means, but by the richest and wealthiest, in a degree involving the truest sacrifice, for the purpose of insuring the attainment of the aims and purposes of the Plan in its present phase of development, are imperative and can brook no delay.

The mighty and laudable effort exerted, by a considerable number of pioneers, in the course of the opening phase of this world-encircling Crusade, in the virgin territories of the globe, must, if this primacy is to remain unimpaired, be increased, doubled, nay trebled, and must manifest itself not only in foreign fields where the prizes so laboriously won during the last twelve months must, at whatever sacrifice, be meticulously preserved, but throughout the entire length and breadth of the American Union, and particularly in the goal cities, where hitherto the work has stagnated, and which must, in the year now entered, become the scene of the finest exploits which the home front has yet seen. A veritable exodus from the large cities where a considerable number of believers have, over a period of years, congregated, both on the Atlantic and Pacific coasts, as well as in the heart of the country, and where, owing to the tempo and the distractions of city life, the progress of the Faith has been retarded, must signalize the inauguration of this most intensive and challenging phase of the Crusade on the home front. Most certainly and emphatically must the lead be given by the two focal centers of Bahá'í activity which rank among the oldest of and occupy the most honored position among, the cities throughout the American Union, the one as the mother city of the North American continent, the other named by 'Abdu'l-Bahá the City of the Covenant. Indeed, so grave are the exigencies of the present hour, and so critical the political position of the country, that were a bare fifteen adult Bahá'ís to be left in each of these cities, over which unsuspected dangers are hanging, it would still be regarded as adequate for the maintenance of their local spiritual assemblies.

WORLD CRUSADE TASKS

While this vital process of multiplication of Bahá'í isolated centers, groups and local assemblies is being accelerated, through a rapid and unprecedented dispersion of believers, and as the result of the initiation of vigorous teaching activities, through individuals as well as administrative agencies, the incorporation of full-fledged local assemblies—a process which has been noticeably slackening in recent years—must be given immediate attention by the community's elected national representatives, reinforcing, thereby, the foundations of local Bahá'í communities, and paving the way for the establishment, in a not too distant future, of local Bahá'í endowments.

The inauguration of the first dependency of the Mashriqu'l-Adhkár, the first link to be forged destined to bind the Community of the Most Great Name to the general public, expectant to witness the first evidences of direct Bahá'í service to humanity as a complement to Bahá'í worship, is yet another task which must be conscientiously tackled and fulfilled in the course of the second phase of this Ten-Year Plan. The consummation of this project must synchronize with the termination of the landscaping of the area surrounding the Temple—a double achievement that will mark yet another stage in the materialization of 'Abdu'l-Bahá's often expressed and cherished hopes for this holiest House of Worship in the Bahá'í world.

Yet another task, of extreme urgency and of great spiritual significance, is the selection and purchase of the site of the future Mashriqu'l-Adhkár in Sweden, as well as the appropriation of sufficient funds during the coming two years, for the establishment, on however modest a scale, of a national Ḥaẓíratu'l-Quds in Anchorage, Alaska, in Panama City and in the capital of Peru, in Suva, in Tokyo and in Johannesburg, and the lending of financial assistance to the Italo-Swiss National Assembly, the proud daughter of the American Bahá'í Community, for the erection of a similar national center in the Italian and Swiss capitals.

Of no less importance, though involving a smaller outlay of funds, is the establishment of token national endowments in the aforementioned cities, in anticipation of the formation of an independent national spiritual assembly in each of them, at a later stage in the execution of this stupendous Plan.

The translation and publication of Bahá'í literature in the European and American Indian languages, allocated to your Assembly and its European Teaching Committee under the provisions of the Ten-Year Plan, is yet another objective of this second phase of this World Crusade, a task that must be resolutely pursued and speedily consummated in order to facilitate the intensive teaching activity which, at a later stage, must be conducted for the purpose of converting a considerable number of the minority races in both Europe and America to the Faith of Bahá'u'lláh.

The all-important teaching enterprises in France and Finland, designed to broaden the basis of the infant Administrative Order in both countries, and extend the ramifications of the Faith to their chief towns and cities, is yet another responsibility which should be promptly discharged, as an indispensable preliminary to the establishment in each of these two countries of an independent national assembly.

Finally, the establishment of a Bahá'í Publishing Trust, similar in its essentials to the institution already functioning in the British Isles, and which must serve as a model for other national assemblies in both the East and the West, is a matter to which prompt and earnest attention must be directed in the course of the second phase of the Plan, and which will require full and speedy consultation with the national elected representatives of the British Bahá'í Community.

A systematic campaign designed to proclaim the Faith to the masses through the press and radio must moreover be launched and maintained with vigilance, persistence and vigor.

The American Bahá'í Community—the champion-builders of an Order which posterity will hail as the harbinger of a civilization to be regarded as the fairest fruit of the Revelation₁ proclaimed by Bahá'u'lláh; the principal trustees of a Plan which future generations will acclaim as one of the two greatest legacies left by the Center of His Covenant; marching in the van of a Crusade which history will recognize as the most momentous spiritual enterprise launched in modern times; beset by the same anxieties and perils by which the nation of which it forms a part finds itself, to an unprecedented degree, afflicted and surrounded—such a community is, at this hour, experiencing the impact of a challenge unique in its sixty years of existence.

CHALLENGE TO EACH INDIVIDUAL BAHÁ'Í

In its meteoric career its fortunes have risen so swiftly, its exploits have so greatly multiplied, its spirit in times of emergency has swelled and risen so high, it has earned on such occasions the applause and excited the admiration of its sister communities throughout both hemispheres to such a degree, that it cannot, at this critical hour in its destinies, suffer this golden opportunity to slip from its grasp, or this priceless privilege to be irretrievably forfeited.

This challenge, so severe and insistent, and yet so glorious, faces no doubt primarily the individual believer on whom, in the last resort, depends the fate of the entire community. He it is who constitutes the warp and woof on which the quality and pattern of the whole fabric must depend. He it is who acts as one of the countless links in the mighty chain that now girdles the globe. He it is who serves as one of the multitude of bricks which support the structure and insure the stability of the administrative edifice now being raised in every part of the world. Without his support, at once whole-hearted, continuous and generous, every measure adopted, and every plan formulated, by the body which acts as the national representative of the community to which he belongs, is foredoomed to failure. The World Center of the Faith itself is paralyzed if such a support on the part of the rank and file of the community is denied it. The Author of the Divine Plan Himself is impeded in His purpose if the proper instruments for the execution of His design are lacking. The sustaining strength of Bahá'u'lláh Himself, the Founder of the Faith, will be withheld from every and each individual who fails in the long run to arise and play his part. The administrative agencies of a divinely conceived Administrative Order at long last erected and relatively perfected stand in dire need of the individual believer to come forward and utilize them with undeviating purpose, serene confidence and exemplary dedication. The heart of the Guardian cannot but leap with joy, and his mind derive fresh inspiration, at every evidence testifying to the response of the individual to his allotted task. The unseen legions, standing rank upon rank, and eager to pour forth from the Kingdom on high the full measure of their celestial strength on the individual participants of this incomparably glorious Crusade, are powerless unless and until each potential crusader decides for himself, and perseveres in his determination, to rush into the arena of service ready to sacrifice his all for the Cause he is called upon to champion.

APPEAL FOR DEDICATION

It is therefore imperative for the individual American believer, and particularly for the affluent, the independent, the comfort-loving and those obsessed by material pursuits, to step forward, and dedicate their resources, their time, their very lives to a Cause of such transcendence that no human eye can even dimly perceive its glory. Let them resolve, instantly and unhesitatingly, to place, each according to his circumstances, his share on the altar of Bahá'í sacrifice, lest, on a sudden, unforeseen calamities rob them of a considerable portion of the earthly things they have amassed.

Now if ever is the time to tread the path which the dawn-breakers of a previous age have so magnificently trodden. Now is the time to carry out, in the spirit and in the letter, the fervent wish so pathetically voiced by 'Abdu'l-Bahá, Who longed, as attested in the Tablets of the

Divine Plan, to "travel though on foot and in the utmost poverty" and raise "in cities, villages, mountains, deserts and oceans" "the call of Yá-Bahá'u'l-Abhá!"

Then, and only then, can the members of this community hasten the advent of the day when, as prophesied by His pen, "heavenly illumination" will "stream" from their country "to all the peoples of the world." Then, and only then will they find themselves "securely established upon the throne of an everlasting dominion."

That the members of this community, of either sex and of every age, of whatever race or background, however limited in experience, capacity and knowledge, may arise as one man, and seize with both hands the God-given opportunities now presented to them through the dispensations of an all-loving, ever-watchful, ever-sustaining Providence, and lend thereby a tremendous impetus to the propelling forces mysteriously guiding the operations of this newly launched, unspeakably potent, world-encompassing Crusade, is one of the dearest wishes which a loving and longing heart holds for them at this great turning point in the fortunes of the Faith of Bahá'u'lláh in the American continent.

[July 28, 1954]

Nine-Pointed Star for Headstone

Approve star for graves.

[October 22, 1954]

(NOTE: The Guardian considered the Greatest Name too sacred for use on tombstones.)

Send Appeals to President Eisenhower

Owing to aggravation of the situation, the hacking to pieces of the bodies of seven believers in the vicinity of Yazd, and the likelihood of worse massacre in the approaching months, advise all groups and assemblies in the United States to address telegraphically President Eisenhower, appealing for his intervention for protection from further massacres of our offenseless, law-abiding co-religionists in Írán and the safeguard of their human rights. Include brief reference to the worst atrocities. National Assembly should address him similar message both in writing and telegraphically. Include list of atrocities in accompanying memorandum . . .

[August 15, 1955]

A Mysterious Dispensation of Providence

PERSECUTION OF THE BAHÁ'ÍS OF ÍRÁN

A crisis in the fortunes of the Faith of Bahá'u'lláh, of exceptional severity, extensive in its ramifications, unpredictable in its immediate consequences, directly involving the overwhelming majority of His followers in the land of His birth, and confronting with a major challenge Bahá'í communities in both hemispheres, has plunged the Bahá'í world, whilst engaged in the prosecution of a world-wide spiritual crusade, into intense sorrow and profound anxiety.

More grievous than any of the intermittent crises which have more or less acutely afflicted the Faith since the inception, over thirty years ago, of the Formative Age of the Bahá'í Dispensation, such as a seizure of the keys of the foremost Shrine of the Bahá'í world by the covenant-breakers residing in the Holy Land; the occupation of the House of Bahá'u'lláh by His traditional enemies in Baghdád; the expropriation of the first Mashriqu'l-Adhkár of the Bahá'í world in Turkistán and the virtual extinction of the 'Ishqábád Bahá'í Community; the disabilities suffered by the Egyptian Bahá'í Community as a result of the verdict of the Egyptian ecclesiastical court and the historic pronouncements of the highest dignitaries of Sunní Islám in Egypt; the defection of the members of 'Abdu'l-Bahá's family and the machinations and eventual deviation of various recognized yet highly ambitious leaders, teachers, as well as administrators, in Persia, Egypt, Germany and the United States—more grievous than any of these, this latest manifestation of the implacable hatred, and relentless opposition, of the as yet firmly entrenched, politically influential avowed adversaries of God's infant Faith, threatens to become more uncontrollable with every passing day.

Indeed in many of its aspects this crisis bears a striking resemblance to the wave of persecutions which periodically swept the cradle of the

Faith in the course of 'Abdu'l-Bahá's ministry, and is tragically reminiscent of the tribulations experienced by the dawn-breakers of the Heroic Age of the Faith at the hour of its birth in that sorely tried, long-agitated land.

With dramatic suddenness, a situation, which had been slowly and secretly developing, came to a head, as the result of the ceaseless intrigue of the fanatical and determined ecclesiastical opponents of the Faith, ever ready to seize their chance, in times of confusion, and to strike mercilessly, at an opportune hour, at the very root of that Faith and of its swiftly developing, steadily consolidating administrative institutions.

The launching of the Crusade itself, with the celebrations and ceremonials which accompanied it; the repercussions of the widely reported proceedings of four successive Intercontinental Teaching Conferences, which heralded its inauguration; the public dedication of the Mother Temple of the West in Wilmette; the systematic intensification of teaching activities in the Arabian Peninsula, enshrining the Qiblih of the entire Islamic world; and, in particular, the opening to the Faith of the twin holy cities of Mecca and Medina—all these may be said to have precipitated this crisis, and alarmed the jealous exponents and guardians of an antiquated religious orthodoxy in the strongholds of both Shí'ah and Sunní Islám.

A PREMEDITATED CAMPAIGN OF PERSECUTION

This premeditated campaign was heralded by violent and repeated public denunciations of the Faith over the air, from the pulpit, and through the press, defaming its holy Founders, distorting its distinctive features, ridiculing its aims and purposes, and perverting its history. It was formally launched by the government's official pronouncement in the Majlis outlawing the Faith and banning its activities throughout the land. It was soon followed by the senseless and uncivilized demolition of the imposing dome of the Bahá'í Central Administrative Headquarters in the capital. It assumed serious proportions through the seizure and occupation of all Bahá'í administrative headquarters throughout the provinces.

This drastic action taken by the representatives of the central authorities in cities, towns and villages was the signal for the loosing of a flood of abuse, accompanied by a series of atrocities simultaneously and shamelessly perpetrated in most of the provinces, bringing in its wake desolation to Bahá'í homes, economic ruin to Bahá'í families, and staining still further the records of Shí'ah Islám in that troubled land.

In Shíráz, in the province of Fárs, the cradle of the Faith, the House of the Báb, ordained by Bahá'u'lláh in His Most Holy Book as the foremost place of pilgrimage in the land of His birth, was twice desecrated, its walls severely damaged, its windows broken and its furniture partly destroyed and carried away. The neighboring house of the Báb's maternal uncle was razed to the ground. Bahá'u'lláh's ancestral home in Tákur, in the province of Mázindarán, the scene of 'Abdu'l-Bahá's early childhood, was occupied. Shops and farms, constituting, in most cases, the sole source of livelihood to peaceful Bahá'í families, were plundered. Crops and livestock, assets patiently acquired by often poor, but always peace-loving, law-abiding farmers, were wantonly destroyed. Bodies in various cemeteries were first disinterred and then viciously mutilated. The homes of rich and poor alike were forcibly entered and ruthlessly looted. Both adults and children were publicly set upon, reviled, beaten and ridiculed. Young women were abducted, and compelled, against their parents' wishes and their own, to marry Muslims. Boys and girls were mobbed at school, mocked and expelled. A boycott, in many cases, was imposed by butchers and bakers, who refused to sell to the adherents of the Faith the barest necessities of life. A girl in her teens was shamelessly raped, whilst an eleven-month-old baby was heartlessly trampled underfoot. Pressure was brought to bear upon the believers to recant their faith and to renounce allegiance to the Cause they had espoused.

Nor was this all. Emboldened by the general applause accorded by the populace to the savage perpetrators of these crimes, a mob of many hundreds marched upon the hamlet of Hurmuzak, to the beating of drums and the sounding of trumpets, and, armed with spades and axes, fell upon a family of seven, the oldest eighty, the youngest nineteen, and, in an orgy of unrestrained fanaticism, literally hacked them to pieces.

Following closely upon this heinous crime, the like of which has not been witnessed since the close of the Heroic Age of the Faith, an official order has been issued by the Prime Minister's office in Ṭihrán, placing an interdiction against the employment of any Bahá'ís in government service, and ordering the instant dismissal of all who insist on adhering to their faith.

Appeals to the Authorities of Írán and to the United Nations

These tragic, swiftly succeeding events have stirred the Bahá'í world to its foundations. Counter measures were immediately taken, and more than a thousand appeals were addressed by national and local assemblies as well as groups in all continents of the globe to the highest authorities in Persia, including the Sháh, in the hope of stemming the tide of persecution threatening to engulf the entire Persian Bahá'í Community. Furthermore, a wide-spread campaign of publicity was initiated in expectation that its repercussions would exert a restraining influence on the perpetrators of these monstrous acts. An appeal was moreover lodged with the Secretary-General of the United Nations, and the President of the Social and Economic Council, copies of which were delivered to the representatives of the member nations of the Council, to the Director of the Human Rights Division, as well as to non-governmental organizations with consultative status. More recently, President Eisenhower, who, as reported in the press, was the first to make mention of the attacks launched against the Faith, was appealed to by the American National Spiritual Assembly as well as by all groups and local assemblies throughout the United States, to intervene on behalf of the victims of these persecutions.

A Wholly Dedicated, Inflexible Resolve

Faced with this organized and vicious onslaught on the followers, the fundamental verities, the shrines and administrative institutions of the Faith of Bahá'u'lláh in the land of His birth, the American Bahá'í Community cannot at this hour relax for a moment in the discharge of the multiple and sacred responsibilities it has pledged itself to fulfill under the Ten-Year Plan and must indeed display a still greater degree of consecration and a nobler spirit of self-sacrifice in the pursuit of the goals it has set itself to achieve.

A wider dispersal throughout the length and breadth of its homeland; a more strenuous effort to consolidate the superb achievements in the newly opened virgin territories in various continents and islands of the globe; a still greater exertion to expedite the translation and publication of Bahá'í literature into the European and American Indian languages assigned to it under the Plan; a more determined thrust towards the vital objectives of acquiring the site of the future Mother Temple of Sweden and of purchasing the remaining national Ḥaẓíratu'l-Quds in the goal countries of Europe, as well as in Central and South America; a concerted endeavor to establish national Bahá'í endowments in these European and Latin American countries; a ceaseless concentration of attention on the incorporation of firmly established local spiritual assemblies throughout the United States and in the goal countries of Europe, and a closer collaboration with the administrative agencies functioning in Europe, Latin America, Africa, Japan and Alaska for the forthcoming formation of the European, Latin American, Southwest African, Japanese and Alaskan national spiritual assemblies; a more intensive campaign to win over to the Faith representatives of American Indian tribes and of the Basque and Gypsy races—above all, a concerted, wholly dedicated, inflexible resolve to win the allegiance of a far greater number of adherents to the Faith it has espoused and to insure a spectacular multiplication of groups, isolated centers and local assemblies in the vast area assigned to its care—through these, more than through anything else, can the American Bahá'í Community—the recognized champion of the persecuted and the down-trodden, and the standard-bearer of the embryonic World Order of Bahá'u'lláh—offset, to a marked degree, the severe losses the Faith has sustained in the land of its birth, and bring an abiding and much needed consolation to the countless hearts that bleed, in this hour of test and trial, throughout the length and breadth of that bitterly troubled land.

"Save the Persecuted Fund"

Not only through its superlative achievements in these diversified and vital spheres of Bahá'í activity, but also through the support given by its members to the "Save the Persecuted Fund" recently established for the succor of the orphaned, the widowed and the dispossessed, and to which the entire Bahá'í world has been invited to contribute, can this stout-hearted, vigilant, self-sacrificing community which on similar past occasions has so nobly discharged its responsibilities, proclaim to an unbelieving and skeptical world, and particularly to its redoubtable, implacable adversaries, the unconquerable spirit which animates it, the inflexible resolve which spurs it on, in the hour of trial, in the service of a Faith to which it stands wholly dedicated.

THE FIRST HOUSE OF WORSHIP IN AFRICA

Over and above such meritorious accomplishments, the members of this community are called upon to demonstrate their solidarity with their sister communities in East and West, and indeed to assert their divinely conferred primacy, through assuming a leading role in providing for the erection of the first Mashriqu'l-Adhkár to be raised in the heart of the African continent—a continent which by virtue of the innumerable exploits which, throughout its length and breadth, colored and white, individuals as well as assemblies, have achieved in recent years, and which, with the sole exception of Australasia, is the only continent deprived of the blessings of such an institution, fully deserves to possess its own independent House of Worship—a House that will gather within its walls members of communities whose prowess has, in the opening years of the second epoch of the Formative Age of the Bahá'í Dispensation, eclipsed the feats performed in both the southern part of the Western Hemisphere and the European continent, and conferred such luster on the annals of our Faith.

Africa, long dormant and neglected, and now stirring in its potential spiritual strength, is, at this very hour, under the eyes of the clamorous multitudes of the adversaries of the Faith pressing for its extirpation in the land of its birth, being called upon to redress the scales so weighed down through the ferocious and ignoble acts of bloodthirsty ecclesiastical oppressors. The erection of such an institution, at such a time, through the combined efforts of the undismayed, undeflected and undefeatable upholders of the Faith of Bahá'u'lláh in both the East and the West, posterity will regard as a worthy answer to the challenge flung down by its bitterest, most powerful and inveterate enemies. Let them give heed to the warnings and admonitions uttered, at an hour of similar danger, by the Founder of the Faith Himself, on the morrow of His third banishment, and addressed in clear and unmistakable language to the "Minister of the Sháh" in Constantinople: "Dost thou believe thou hast the power to frustrate His will, to hinder Him from executing His judgment, or to deter Him from exercising His sovereignty? Pretendest thou that aught in the heavens or in the earth can resist His Faith? No, by Him Who is the eternal

Truth! Nothing whatsoever in the whole of creation can thwart His purpose. . . . Know thou, moreover, that He it is Who hath by His own behest, created all that is in the heavens and all that is on the earth. How can, then, the thing that hath been created at His bidding prevail against Him?"

A Blessing in Disguise

Indeed this fresh ordeal that has, in pursuance of the mysterious dispensations of Providence, afflicted the Faith, at this unexpected hour, far from dealing a fatal blow to its institutions or existence, should be regarded as a blessing in disguise, not a "calamity" but a "providence" of God, not a devastating flood but a "gentle rain" on a "green pasture," a "wick" and "oil" unto the "lamp" of His Faith, a "nurture" for His Cause, "water for that which has been planted in the hearts of men," a "crown set on the head" of His Messenger for this Day.

Whatever its outcome, this sudden commotion that has seized the Bahá'í world, that has revived the hopes and emboldened the host of the adversaries of the Faith intent on quenching its light and obliterating it from the face of the earth, has served as a trumpet call in the sounding of which the press of the world, the cries of its vociferous enemies, the public remonstrances of both men of good will and those in authority have joined, proclaiming far and wide its existence, publicizing its history, defending its verities, unveiling its truths, demonstrating the character of its institutions and advertising its aims and purposes.

Unprecedented Publicity

Seldom, if at any time since its inception, has such a widespread publicity been accorded the infant Faith of God, now at long last emerging from an obscurity which has so long and so grievously oppressed it. Not even the dramatic execution of its Herald, nor the blood-bath which, in circumstances of fiendish cruelty followed quickly in its wake in the city of Ṭihrán, nor even the widely advertised travels of the Center of Bahá'u'lláh's Covenant in the West, succeeded in focusing the attention of the world and in inviting the notice of those in high places as has this latest manifestation of God's inscrutable will, this marvelous demonstration of His invincible power, this latest move in His Own Major Plan, using both the mighty and lowly as pawns in His world-shaping game, for the fulfillment of His immediate purpose and the eventual establishment of His Kingdom on earth.

For though the newly launched World Spiritual Crusade, constituting at best only the Minor Plan in the execution of the Almighty's design for the redemption of mankind—has, as a result of this turmoil, paralyzing temporarily the vast majority of the organized followers of Bahá'u'lláh within His birthplace, suffered a severe setback—yet the over-all Plan of God, moving mysteriously and in contrast to the orderly and well-known processes of a clearly devised Plan, has received an impetus the force of which only posterity can adequately assess.

A Faith, which, for a quarter of a century, has, in strict accordance with the provisions of the Will and Testament of 'Abdu'l-Bahá, been building its Administrative Order—the embryonic World Order of Bahá'u'lláh—through the laborious erection of its local and national administrative institutions; which set out, in the opening years of the second epoch of this Formative Age, through the launching of a series of national Plans as well as a World Crusade, to utilize the machinery of its institutions, created patiently and unobtrusively in the course of the first epoch of that Age, for the systematic propagation of its teachings in all the continents and chief islands of the globe—such a Faith finds itself, whilst in the midst of discharging its second and vital task, thrust into the limelight of an unprecedented publicity—a publicity which its followers never anticipated, which will involve them in fresh and inescapable responsibilities, and which will, no doubt, reinforce the tasks which they have undertaken, in recent years, to discharge.

To the intensification of such a publicity in which non-Bahá'í agencies and even the avowed adversaries of the Faith are playing so active a part, the members of the American Bahá'í Community, the outstanding defenders of the Faith, blessed with a freedom so cruelly denied the vast majority of their brethren, and equipped with the means and instruments needed to make that publicity effective, must fully and decisively contribute. The echoes of the mighty trumpet blast, now so providentially sounded, awakening a multitude of the ignorant and the skeptical, both high and low, to the existence and significance of the Message of Bahá'u'lláh, must under no circumstances, and at such a propitious hour, be allowed to die out.

Nay, their reverberations must be followed up by further calls designed to proclaim, in still more resounding tones, the aims and tenets of this glorious Cause, and to expose, whilst avoiding any attack on the ruling authorities, even more convincingly than before, the barbarous ferocity of the acts which have been perpetrated, as well as the odious fanaticism which has inspired such conduct.

Strenuous and urgent as is the task falling to the lot of a community already so over-burdened with a multiplicity of unavoidable obligations, the possibilities involved in the assumption of this supplementary responsibility are truly tremendous, the benefits that are destined to accrue from its proper discharge are immense, and the reward inestimably rich.

Let them remember, as they pursue diligently this sacred task, that such a publicity, following closely upon such dire tribulations, afflicting so large a number of their brethren, in so sacred a land, cannot but prove to be a prelude, however slow the process involved, to the emancipation of these same valiant sufferers from the galling fetters of an antiquated religious orthodoxy, which, great as has been its decline in the course of over a century, still wields considerable power and exercises a widespread influence in high circles as well as among the masses. Such an emancipation, which cannot be confined to Bahá'u'lláh's native land, will, in varying measure, have its repercussions in Islamic countries, or may be even preceded by a similar phenomenon in neighboring territories, hastening and adding fresh impetus to the bursting of the bonds that fetter the freedom of the followers of God's infant Faith.

WORLD RECOGNITION OF THE FAITH

Such a consummation will, in its turn, pave the way for the recognition of that Faith as an independent religion established on a basis of absolute equality with its sister religions, enjoying the unqualified protection of the civil authorities for its followers and its institutions, and fully empowered, in all matters related to personal status, to apply without any reservations the laws and ordinances ordained in the Most Holy Book.

That the members of the American Bahá'í Community—the outstanding protagonists of the Cause of God; the stout-hearted defenders of its integrity, its claims and its rights, the champion-builders of its

Administrative Order; the standard-bearers of its crusading hosts; the torchbearers of its embryonic civilization; the chief succorers of the down-trodden, the needy and the fettered among its followers—that the members of such a community, may, whilst discharging, fully and unflinchingly, their specific tasks in accordance with the provisions of the Ten-Year Plan, seize the present God-sent opportunity, and hasten, through a proper discharge of this supplementary task, the consummation of such ardent hopes for so signal a victory, is a prayer constantly in my heart, and a wish which I treasure above all others.

[August 20, 1955]

Revitalize Entire Community

Urge intensification of efforts to revitalize entire community and expedite attainment of plans and objectives, particularly as related to purchase of Ḥaẓíras and endowments in America and Europe; translation into remaining languages; incorporation of assemblies; multiplication of centers and assemblies on home front; opening of Iceland, Spitzbergen, Anticosti and remaining islands of Pacific and Atlantic. Fervently supplicating for immediate signal victories.

[January 5, 1956]

Greater Consecration to Pressing Tasks

Deplore situation on home front. Praying ardently for rededication of entire community for greater consecration to pressing tasks. Approve all suggestions in recent letter. Urge that you redouble efforts, supplicate for unprecedented blessings.

[February 2, 1956]

Praying for Great Victories on Home Front

Fervently praying for great victories on the home front. Appeal to entire community to arise, participate and insure attainment of goals.

[June 22, 1956]

Inestimable Prizes Within Our Reach

As I survey, after the lapse of a little over three years, the vast range of historic and unforgettable achievements with which the stout-hearted, high-minded and wholly consecrated followers of the Faith of Bahá'u'lláh have, in the course of the operations of a World Spiritual Crusade, enriched, in every continent of the globe and in so many islands of the seven seas, the annals of the Formative Age of His Dispensation, I cannot but acknowledge, with feelings of pride, of joy, and of gratitude, the preponderating share which the American Bahá'í Community, faithful to its traditions, and in keeping with its high standard of stewardship to the Cause of God, has had in the conduct of this world-encircling enterprise and the discharge of its manifold, its pressing and sacred responsibilities. With one or two exceptions, greatly to be deplored, this valiant community has, ever since the inception of this Spiritual Crusade, and in every sphere of Bahá'í activities in which its participators have both individually and collectively been assiduously engaged, set an example of whole-hearted dedication, dogged perseverance, unstinting self-sacrifice and undeviating loyalty worthy of emulation by its sister, as well as its daughter, communities over the entire face of the globe.

The number, the character and the rapidity of the spiritual conquests achieved by its steadfast and intrepid members, in so many sovereign states of the globe, its chief dependencies and widely scattered islands, in the course of the one-year period, constituting the opening phase of a memorable Plan, will no doubt be universally acclaimed as a turning point of unimaginable consequence in Bahá'í history. Such feats, in so many territories, during so short a time, will rank, in the eyes of posterity, as superb and outstanding exploits, immortalizing the fame of the American followers of the Faith of Bahá'u'lláh, and as epoch-making events unsurpassed since the closing of the Heroic Age of the Bahá'í Dispensation.

Aid Accorded to Their Oppressed Brethren in Persia

The reaction, so swift and so energetic, of the members of this same community, now deservedly recognized as the impregnable citadel of the Faith of God, and the cradle of the rising institutions of its World

Order, to the sudden onslaught made upon the institutions, the lives and the livelihood of their oppressed brethren, members of the numerically leading and the most venerable national Bahá'í community, by the traditonal adversaries of a long-persecuted Faith, has been such as to deepen, to a marked extent, the feelings of genuine admiration and esteem, so strongly felt throughout the Bahá'í world, for the enduring and magnificent services rendered in the course of more than six decades by the American believers to the Faith of Bahá'u'lláh and its embryonic World Order. The spontaneity with which the rank and file of this community as well as the body of its elected representatives, have contributed to the "Save the Persecuted Fund" established for the succor of the victims of these savage and periodically recurring barbarities; the measure of publicity accorded them in the American press, as well as over the radio; the timely and efficacious intervention of men of prominence, in various walks of life, on behalf of the oppressed and the down-trodden; the repeated and direct appeals addressed by them to the highest authorities in Persia, as well as to their representative in the United States; the immense number of written and cabled appeals, made by the local as well as the national elected representatives of the community, to the chief magistrate of Persia, his ministers and parliament; the numerous messages addressed by the same representatives to the chief executive of the United States, urging his personal intervention, the pleading of the cause of an harassed, sorely-tried community in the course of repeated representations made to the State Department in Washington; the part played in the presentation of the Bahá'í case to the United Nations officials in both Geneva and New York; the allocation of a sizeable sum for the purpose of securing the assistance of an expert publicity agent, in order to reinforce the publicity already being received in the public press—these, as well as other measures which, by their very nature, must of necessity remain confidential—proclaim, in no uncertain terms, the dynamic and decisive nature of the aid accorded, in a hour of trial and emergency, by the champions of the Faith of Bahá'u'lláh, raised up in the great republic of the West, at such a crucial hour in the evolution of His Plan, for both His Faith and the world at large, to the vast body of the descendants of the dawn-breakers of the Apostolic Age of that same Faith in the land of its birth.

A Noble Record of Service

No less remarkable has been the share of this community, chiefly responsible, on the morrow of 'Abdu'l-Bahá's passing, for the fixing of the pattern, the elaboration of the national constitution, and the erection of the basic institutions, of a divinely conceived Administrative Order, in the acquisition and establishment, in the course of two brief years, constituting the second phase of the Ten-Year Plan, of practically all of the future national administrative headquarters—numbering over thirty—of Bahá'í national assemblies in four continents of the globe, involving the expenditure from the National Fund of over a hundred thousand dollars.

An effort, hardly less meritorious and equally efficacious and astonishing, has been exerted by the members of this alert, forward-looking, ceaselessly laboring community, in the course of the same two-year period, for the establishment of national Bahá'í endowments in more than twenty countries of both the Eastern and Western Hemi-spheres, entailing the expenditure of over twenty thousand dollars.

In other spheres of Bahá'í activity, related to the prosecution of the Ten-Year Plan, all of vital importance to the teaching work initiated under that same Plan, and to the enlargement and consolidation of the administrative structure of the institutions to be erected in the future, the accomplishments of the members of this community, during the first two phases of this world Crusade, have been no less significant. The establishment of the Bahá'í Publishing Trust; the translation of Bahá'í literature into more than fifteen languages, both within the scope of the Ten-Year Plan and outside it, spoken in Europe, Asia, Latin America and the North American continent; the purchase of the site of the first dependency of the Mother Temple of the West; the practical completion of the landscaping of its gardens; the provision of a considerable part of the material resources required for the purchase of the sites of future Bahá'í Temples in both the Eastern and Western Hemispheres, as well as for the construction of the two projected Mashriqu'l-Adhkárs in the European and African continents; the guidance given and the aid extended to newly elected national assemblies, for the efficient conduct of Bahá'í administrative activities and the prosecution of Bahá'í national plans; the initial visits made by Bahá'í teachers to countries within the Soviet orbit, foreshadowing the launching of systematic teaching enterprises in both Europe and Asia; the assistance given, through financial help as well as through the dispatch of Bahá'í pioneers, to various Bahá'í communities for the enlargement of the limits of the Faith and the consolidation of its institutions; and, last but not least, the purchase of the sacred site of the Síyáh-Chál of Ṭihrán, the scene of the birth of Bahá'u'lláh's Prophetic Mission, by a member of that community of Persian descent—these stand out as further evidences of the enormous share the firmly knit, highly organized, swiftly advancing, fully dedicated American Bahá'í Community has had in the prosecution and triumphant progress of the three year old Ten-Year Plan, and augur well for a no less splendid contribution to be made, in the years immediately ahead, for the attainment of its remaining objectives.

FRUITFUL EFFORTS OF HANDS OF THE CAUSE

Supplementing this noble record of service have been the constant and fruitful efforts exerted by the Hands of the Cause, nominated from among the members of that community, in both the United States and the Holy Land, efforts that have lent a considerable impetus to the expansion and consolidation of the far-reaching enterprises initiated at the World Center of the Faith, and which have, particularly through the instrumentality of the recently appointed American Auxiliary Board, stimulated, to a noticeable extent the progress of the teaching work and the advancement of the Plan itself.

STUPENDOUS WORK ACHIEVED BY MEMBERS OF THE INTERNATIONAL BAHÁ'Í COUNCIL

Particular tribute should, I feel, at this juncture, be paid to the stupendous work achieved, since the launching of the World Crusade, by the representatives of this highly privileged community, in their capacity as members of the International Bahá'í Council, in connection with the prosecution of a variety of enterprises embarked upon in recent years, aiming at the expansion and consolidation of the international institutions of the Faith, the enhancement of its prestige, the embellishment of the surroundings of its Shrines, the efficient conduct of its internal affairs, and the forging of fresh links binding it still more closely to the civil authorities in the Holy Land. The erection of the International Archives in the close neighborhood of the Báb's holy Sepulcher; the extension of the international Bahá'í endowments on the slopes of Mt. Carmel; the formation of several Israel Branches of Bahá'í National Spiritual Assemblies; the embellishment of the precincts of the resting-place of both the Báb and Bahá'u'lláh; the purchase of the site of the first Mashriqu'l-Adhkár of the Holy Land; the preparation of the designs for the International Bahá'í Archives on Mt. Carmel; and of the Mother Temples of Persia and of Africa; the inauguration of the preliminary steps for the eventual construction of Bahá'u'lláh's holy Sepulcher; the measures adopted, with the assistance of various officials of the State of Israel, for the eviction of the covenant-breakers from the immediate precincts of the Shrine of Bahá'u'lláh and the elimination of any influence they still exercise, after the lapse of over sixty years, in the close vicinity of that Most Holy Spot—in these, as well as in other various subsidiary activities, constantly increasing in number as well as in diversity at the spiritual and administrative center of the Bahá'í world, have the members of the little band, assiduously laboring under the shadow of the Holy Shrines, and befittingly representing the American Bahá'í Community, conspicuously participated, and through their dedicated services, added fresh luster to the annals of the community to which they belong.

REVITALIZATION OF THE HOME FRONT

So splendid a record of service, rendered within the brief span of a little over three years, extending over so vast an area of the globe, so highly diversified, so pregnant with promise, in the face of such formidable obstacles, and by so limited a number of participants, has, much to my deepest regret, been marred by a progressive devitalization of the home front, constituting so momentous an aspect of the Ten-Year Plan, and upon which its continued and effective prosecution by the American Bahá'í Community, in the course of the present and third phase of the World Spiritual Crusade, so largely depends.

Constituting as it does the base of the multiple operations now being conducted to ensure the success of the North American, the Latin American, the African, the European and Asiatic campaigns of a global crusade, no sacrifice can be deemed too great for its revitalization and the broadening and consolidation of its foundations. The manpower of the community, so essential to the further deployment of its forces must, rapidly and at all costs, increase. The material resources, now at its disposal, which are so bountifully poured forth and so generously distributed to the four corners of the globe, must be correspondingly augmented to meet the pressing and ever-swelling demands of a constantly and irresistibly advancing Crusade. A far greater proportion of the avowed supporters of the Faith must arise, ere the Crusade suffers any setback, for the fourfold purpose of winning over an infinitely greater number of recruits to the army of Bahá'u'lláh fighting on the home front, of swelling to an unprecedented degree the isolated centers now scattered within its confines, of converting an increasing number of them into firmly founded groups, and of accelerating the formation of local assemblies, while safeguarding those already in existence.

The Individual Bahá'í Must Arise

There can be no doubt whatever that to achieve this fourfold purpose is the most strenuous, the least spectacular, and the most challenging of the tasks now confronting the American Bahá'í Community. It is primarily a task that concerns the individual believer, wherever he may be, and whatever his calling, his resources, his race, or his age. Neither the local nor national representatives of the community, no matter how elaborate their plans, or persistent their appeals, or sagacious their counsels, nor even the Guardian himself, however much he may yearn for this consummation, can decide where the duty of the individual lies, or supplant him in the discharge of that task. The individual alone must assess its character, consult his conscience, prayerfully consider all its aspects, manfully struggle against the natural inertia that weighs him down in his effort to arise, shed, heroically and irrevocably, the trivial and superfluous attachments which hold him back, empty himself of every thought that may tend to obstruct his path, mix, in obedience to the counsels of the Author of His Faith, and in imitation of the One Who is its true Exemplar, with men and women, in all walks of life, seek to touch their hearts, through the distinction which characterizes his thoughts, his words and his acts, and win them over tactfully, lovingly, prayerfully and persistently, to the Faith he himself has espoused.

The gross materialism that engulfs the entire nation at the present hour; the attachment to worldly things that enshrouds the souls of men; the fears and anxieties that distract their minds; the pleasure and dissipations that fill their time, the prejudices and animosities that darken their outlook, the apathy and lethargy that paralyze their spiritual faculties—these are among the formidable obstacles that stand in the path of every would-be warrior in the service of Bahá'u'lláh, obstacles which he must battle against and surmount in his crusade for the redemption of his own countrymen.

To the degree that the home front crusader is himself cleansed of these impurities, liberated from these petty preoccupations and gnawing anxieties, delivered from these prejudices and antagonisms, emptied of self, and filled by the healing and the sustaining power of God, will he be able to combat the forces arrayed against him, magnetize the souls of those whom he seeks to convert, and win their unreserved, their enthusiastic and enduring allegiance to the Faith of Bahá'u'lláh.

Delicate and strenuous though the task may be, however arduous and prolonged the effort required, whatsoever the nature of the perils and pitfalls that beset the path of whoever arises to revive the fortunes of a Faith struggling against the rising forces of materialism, nationalism, secularism, racialism, ecclesiasticism, the all-conquering potency of the grace of God, vouchsafed through the Revelation of Bahá'u'lláh, will, undoubtedly, mysteriously and surprisingly, enable whosoever arises to champion His Cause to win complete and total victory.

The history of a century-old Faith eloquently bears witness to similar unnumbered successes won, in both the Apostolic and Formative Ages of the Bahá'í Dispensation, in circumstances even more challenging than those in which the American Bahá'í Community now finds itself.

So magnificent a victory, won collectively, at such a time, in a country so vitally affecting the immediate destinies of mankind, singled out to play so predominant a role in the unification and spiritualization of the entire human race, by a community which in every other field can boast a brilliant and unbroken record of victories, will, no doubt, exert not only a profound influence on the ultimate destinies of an entire nation and people, but will galvanize, through its repercussions, the entire Bahá'í world.

"A Prayer Which I Never Cease to Utter"

The prizes within the reach of this community are truly inestimable. Much will depend on the reaction of the rank and file of the believers to the plea now addressed to them with all the fervor of my soul.

To act, and act promptly and decisively, is the need of the present hour and their inescapable duty. That the American Bahá'í Community may, in this one remaining field, where so much is at stake, and where the needs of the Faith are so acute, cover itself with a glory that will outshine the splendor of its past exploits in the far-flung territories of the globe, is a prayer which I never cease to utter in my continual supplications to Bahá'u'lláh.

[July 19, 1956]

Intensification of Efforts

Welcome pledge by delegates. Fervently supplicating Bahá'u'lláh's sustaining grace. Urge intensification of efforts, rededication and achievement of goals of Plan in order to discharge befittingly the sacred, manifold, inescapable, urgent responsibilities confronting the entire American Bahá'í Community. Appeal for unprecedented increase in pioneers on the home front and all continents of the globe, on which the prosperity, security and destiny of the American believers must ultimately rest.

[April 29, 1957]

Dual, Inescapable, Paramount Responsibilities

Assembly's dual, inescapable, paramount responsibilities for current year are to ensure expansion and consolidation of the home front and the rapid multiplication of pioneers abroad to reinforce Latin American, African, European and Pacific campaigns of World Crusade. Fervently supplicating for signal success in fulfillment of dearest hopes.

[May 7, 1957]

Heights Never Before Attained

The American Bahá'í Community has, ever since the launching of the global Spiritual Crusade, in which it has been assigned the lion's share in view of the primacy conferred upon it by 'Abdu'l-Bahá, exerted itself, in numerous and widely scattered areas of the globe, with commendable perseverance, a high sense of undeviating loyalty and exemplary consecration. The inexorable march of events, hastening its members along the path of their destiny, is steadily carrying them to the stage at which the momentous Plan, to which they have dedicated their resources, will have reached its midway point.

Enduring Achievements

A prodigious expenditure of effort, a stupendous flow of material resources, an unprecedented dispersal of pioneers, embracing so vast a section of the globe, and bringing in their wake the rise, the multiplication and consolidation of so many institutions, so divers in character, so potent and full of promise, already stand to their credit, and augur well for a befitting consummation of a decade-long task in the years immediately ahead.

The opening of a large percentage of the virgin territories, scattered over the face of the planet, and assigned, under the provisions of the Ten-Year Plan, to this community and its sister and daughter communities in all continents of the globe; the allocation of vast sums, for the founding of national Ḥaẓíratu'l-Quds, for the establishment of national Bahá'í endowments; and for the purchase of the sites of future Bahá'í Temples; the financial aid extended and the moral support accorded to a still persecuted sister community, struggling heroically for its emancipation, in the cradle of the Faith; the steady progress in the vital process of incorporating firmly grounded local spiritual assemblies in various states of the union; the translation of Bahá'í literature into the languages listed in the Ten-Year Plan, as well as into a number of supplementary languages, spontaneously undertaken by American Bahá'í pioneers in territories far beyond the confines of their homeland; the completion of the landscaping of the area immediately surrounding the Mother Temple of the West, in conformity with the expressed, often repeated wishes of 'Abdu'l-Bahá, contributing so greatly to the beauty of an edifice, the spiritual influence of which He, repeatedly and unequivocally, emphasized; the acquisition of the site of the first dependency of that same edifice, designed to pave the way for the early establishment of the first of several institutions, which, as conceived by Him, will be grouped around every Bahá'í House of Worship, complementing, through their association with direct service to mankind, in the educational, the humanitarian and social fields, its spiritual function as the ordained place of communion with the Creator and the Spirit of His appointed Messenger in this day; the establishment of the Bahá'í Publishing Trust; the generous financial assistance extended, the administrative guidance vouchsafed and the unfailing encouragement given, by the elected representatives of this same community to the newly fledged assemblies, emerging into independent existence in both the Eastern and Western Hemispheres; the substantial share which one of its members has had in the acquisition of one of the holy sites in the capital city of Bahá'u'lláh's native land; the preponderating role played by the various agencies, acting under the direction of its national elected representatives, in giving publicity to the Faith, through the proclamation of the fundamental verities underlying the Bahá'í Revelation, the airing of the manifold grievances weighing so heavily on the overwhelming majority of their coreligionists, and the appeals directed, on their behalf, to men of eminence in various walks of life, as well as to different departments of the United Nations, both in New York and Geneva; and, finally, ranking as equally meritorious to anything hitherto achieved by the members of this privileged community, the magnificent and imperishable contribution made by them, singly and collectively, to the rise and establishment of the institutions of their beloved Faith at its World Center; through the assistance given by their distinguished representatives serving in the Holy Land, in hastening the erection of the Bahá'í International Archives, through the purchase of the site of the Mother Temple of the Holy Land, the enlargement of the scope of Bahá'í international endowments on the slopes of Mt. Carmel and in the Plain of 'Akká, the embellishment of the sacred precincts of the two holiest Shrines of the Bahá'í world; the formation of the Israel Branches of four national spiritual assemblies, the preparation and completion of the designs of the first Mashriqu'l-Adhkárs to be erected in the Asiatic, the African and Australian continents, and the setting in motion, through the instrumentality of various departments of the Israeli government, of a long-drawn-out process, culminating in the expropriation by the state of the entire property, owned and controlled by the remnants of the breakers of Bahá'u'lláh's Covenant, immediately surrounding His resting-place and the Mansion of Bahjí, the evacuation of this property by this ignoble band, and the final and definite purification, after the lapse of no less than six decades, of the Outer Sanctuary of the Most Holy Shrine of the Bahá'í world, of the defilement, which had caused so much sorrow and anxiety to the heart of 'Abdu'l-Bahá—these are among the enduring achievements which four brief years of unremitting devotion to the interests of the Ten-Year Plan have brought about, and which will eternally redound to the glory of the champion-builders of Bahá'u'lláh's embryonic World Order, holding aloft so valiantly the banner of His Faith in the great republic of the West.

THE HOME FRONT—BASE FOR EXPANSION OF FUTURE OPERATIONS

Though much has been achieved in the space of less than five years, though the objectives of the Ten-Year Plan, in most of its essential aspects, may be said to have been triumphantly attained long before the time appointed for its termination, through a striking display, and a remarkable combination, of American Bahá'í initiative, resourcefulness, generosity, fidelity and perseverance, the Plan, prosecuted hitherto so vigorously by the rank and file of this community, may be said to be still suffering in some of its vital aspects, from certain deficiencies, which, if not speedily and fundamentally remedied, will not only mutilate the Plan itself, but jeopardize the prizes won so laboriously since its inauguration.

As I have already forewarned the energetic prosecutors of the global Crusade in the North American continent, the home front, from which have sprung, since the inception of the Formative Age of the Faith, the dynamic forces which have set in motion, and directed the operation, of so many processes, in both the teaching and administrative spheres of Bahá'í activity, and which must continue to act as a base for the steady expansion of future operations in every continent of the globe, and the extension of their ramifications to the uttermost corners of the earth, and which must be increasingly regarded, as the forces of internal disruption and the stress and danger of aggressiveness from without gather momentum, as the sole stronghold of a Faith which cannot hope to escape unscathed from the turmoil gathering around it—such a home front must, at all costs, and in the shortest possible time, be spiritually reinvigorated, administratively expanded, and materially replenished. The flame of devotion ignited and the enthusiasm generated, during the celebrations which commemorated the centenary of the birth of the Mission of the Divine Author of our Faith, and which, in the course of the years immediately following it have carried the members of the American Bahá'í Community, so far and so high, along the road leading to their ultimate destiny, must, in whatever way possible, be fanned and continually fed throughout the entire area of the Union, in every state from the Atlantic to the Pacific seaboards, in every locality where Bahá'ís reside, in every heart throbbing with the love of Bahá'u'lláh. The spirit that sent forth, not so long ago, in such rapid succession, so many pioneers to such remote areas of the globe, must at all costs and above everything else, be recaptured, for the two-fold purpose of swelling the number, and of ensuring the continual flow, of pioneers, so essential for the safeguarding of the prizes won in the course of the several campaigns of a world-girdling Crusade, and of combatting the evil forces which a relentless and all-pervasive materialism, the cancerous growth of militant racialism, political corruption, unbridled capitalism, wide-spread lawlessness and gross immorality, are, alas, unleashing, with ominous swiftness, amongst various classes of the society to which the members of this community belong.

The administrative strongholds of a Faith, bound to be subjected on the one hand, to a severe spiritual challenge from within, through the inevitable impact of these devastating influences on its infant strength, and, on the other, to the onslaught of ecclesiastical leaders, the traditional defenders of religious orthodoxy from without, must be multiplied and reinforced for the purpose of warding off the inevitable attacks of the assailants, of vindicating the ideals and principles which animate their defenders, and of ensuring the ultimate victory and ascendency of the Faith itself over the nefarious elements seeking to undermine it from within, and its powerful detractors aiming at its extinction from without.

Nor must the material resources, so vitally required to meet the challenge of a continually expanding Faith, be, for a moment, either ignored, neglected, or underestimated—resources which a home front, materially and adequately replenished by a steady and marked influx of active and wholehearted supporters from all ranks of society, can, in the long run, provide. As the imperative needs of a Faith, now irresistibly advancing in every direction, multiply, a corresponding increase in the financial means at the disposal of its national administrators directing and controlling its operations, within and beyond the confines of their homeland, to meet these essential and urgent requirements, must be ensured, if its onward march is not to be either halted or slowed down.

MIGHTY AND HISTORIC ENTERPRISES

It is upon the individual believer, constituting the fundamental unit in the structure of the home front, that the revitalization, the expansion, and the enrichment of the home front must ultimately depend. The more strenuous the effort exerted, daily and methodically, by the individual laboring on the home front to rise to loftier heights of consecration, of self-abnegation, to contribute, through pioneering at home, to the multiplication of Bahá'í isolated centers, groups and assemblies, and to raise, through diligent, painstaking and continual endeavor to convert receptive souls to the Faith he has espoused, the number of its active and wholehearted supporters, the sooner will the vast and multiple enterprises, launched beyond the confines of the homeland, and now so desperately calling for a greater supply of men and means, be provided with the necessary support that will ensure their uninterrupted development and hasten their ultimate fruition, and the lighter will be the burden of the impending contest that must be waged, sooner or later, within the borders of the Union itself, between the rising institutions of Bahá'u'lláh's embryonic divinely appointed Order, and the exponents of obsolescent doctrines and the defenders, both secular and religious, of a corrupt and fast-declining society.

The fourth phase of the Ten-Year Plan, which the prosecutors of a world-encompassing Crusade are about to enter, *must witness on the one hand*, on every home front, and particularly within the confines of the American homeland, *this same spiritual reinvigoration, administrative expansion*, and *material replenishment, constituting the triple facets* of a task which can brook no further delay, and, on the other, *an acceleration, particularly in connection with the construction of the Mother Temples of Australia and Germany* (the needs of the Mother Temple of Africa having, to all intents and purposes, been met) *in the contributions to be made, by individual believers as well as national spiritual assemblies, to ensure the uninterrupted progress and the early completion of these mighty and historic enterprises.*

As the members of the valiant American Bahá'í Community have, in the space of more than four years, blazed the trail, and vindicated their primacy, through the share they have had in opening the chief remaining virgin territories of the globe, in contributing to the furtherance of the interests of the institutions of the Faith at its World Center, and in hastening the acquisition of national Ḥaẓíratu'l-Quds, the establishment of Bahá'í national endowments, and the purchase of sites for future Bahá'í Temples, so must they, if they be intent on safeguarding that primacy, and on preserving, intact and untarnished, the noble example they have already set the Bahá'í world, maintain their enviable position, as the vanguard of the army of Bahá'u'lláh's crusaders, in rescuing, while there is yet time, their home front from the precarious position in which it now finds itself, and in displaying for the purpose of ensuring the erection of the Mother Temples of three continents—tasks which tower far above any of the national enterprises hitherto undertaken—be they Ḥaẓíratu'l-Quds, endowments or Temple sites—that selfsame generosity and self-abnegation which have distinguished their stewardship to the Cause of Bahá'u'lláh in the past.

The year, the opening of which will mark the midway point of this World Spiritual Crusade, must be distinguished from all previous years, by the special allotment of a substantial sum from the national budget that will adequately meet the urgent needs of these Houses of Worship, and particularly those that are to be erected in the European and Australian continents.

A Golden Opportunity, a Glorious Challenge

The forthcoming convocation of no less than five intercontinental conferences, marking the passing of half of the time allotted for the prosecution of a World Crusade, and to be held, in five continents of the globe, for the purpose of paying homage to the Author of the Bahá'í Revelation for His protection, guidance and blessings, of focusing attention on the achievements of the immediate past and the pressing requirements of the immediate future, will, it is my ardent hope and prayer, provide a fresh stimulus for the adequate discharge of these two afore-mentioned responsibilities, which constitute the distinguishing features of the fourth phase of a rapidly unfolding Plan.

At four of these five conferences, in the proceedings of which four, the members of the American Bahá'í Community—the principal executors of 'Abdu'l-Bahá's Divine Plan and the keepers and defenders of the stronghold of the Bahá'í Administrative Order—will participate, through their official representatives, the voice of the champion-builders of Bahá'u'lláh's embryonic World Order, who can well claim to have had a decisive share in the great strides made by this Crusade, should be raised in a spirit and manner that will galvanize these conferences into action, and produce such results as will reverberate round the world.

A golden opportunity, a glorious challenge, an inescapable duty, a staggering responsibility, confront them, at this fresh turning point in the fortunes of a Crusade, for which they have so unremittingly labored, whose Cause they have so notably advanced, in the further unfoldment of which they must continue to play a leading part, and in whose closing stages, they will, I feel confident, rise to heights never before attained in the course of six decades of American Bahá'í history.

Once again—and this time more fervently than ever before—I direct my plea to every single member of this strenuously laboring, clear-visioned, stout-hearted, spiritually endowed community, every man and woman, on whose individual efforts, resolution, self-sacrifice and perserverance the immediate destinies of the Faith of God, now traversing so crucial a stage in its rise and establishment, primarily depends, not to allow, through apathy, timidity or complacency, this one remaining opportunity to be irretrievably lost. I would rather entreat each and every one of them to immortalize this approaching, fateful hour in the evolution of a World Spiritual Crusade, by a fresh consecration to their God-given mission, coupled with an instantaneous plan of action, at once so dynamic and decisive, as to wipe out, on the one hand, with one stroke, the deficiencies which have, to no small extent, bogged down the operations of the Crusade on the home front, and tremendously accelerate, on the other, the progress of the triple task, launched, in three continents, and constituting one of its preeminent objectives.

His Watchful Power and Unfailing Grace

May He, Who through the irresistible operation of the will of His almighty Father, called this community into being, nursed it in its infancy through the inestimable benefits conferred by a divinely appointed Covenant, infused through His personal contact with its members, and the proclamation of His Own Station, a new spirit into their souls; conferred, subsequently, through the revelation of His Tablets, the spiritual primacy designed to enable them to assume a preponderating role in the propagation of His Father's Faith; graciously aided them, following His ascension, to inaugurate their God-given mission by fixing the pattern, creating the institutions, and vindicating the purpose, of a divinely appointed Administrative Order and by launching subsequently the preliminary undertakings in their home-land, as well as in all the republics of Latin America, in anticipation of the formal inauguration of a systematic World Crusade for the further-ance of His Father's Cause; and more recently assisted them to embark, in concert with their brethren in other continents of the globe, upon the first stage of their world-encompassing mission, and to win a series of victories unprecedented in the annals of the Faith in their homeland—may He, through His watchful care and unfailing grace, continue to sustain them, individually and collectively, in the course of the remaining stages of the Plan, and enable them to bring to a triumphant termination the initial epoch in the unfoldment of the Divine Plan which He has primarily entrusted to them and on the successful prosecution of which their entire spiritual destiny must depend.

[September 21, 1957]

IN MEMORIAM

Frank Ashton

Praying for progress of his soul in the Kingdom. His services meritorious.

[March 1956]

Ella Bailey

Grieve at passing of valiant exemplary pioneer. Reward in Kingdom bountiful.

[August 30, 1953]

Dorothy Baker

Hearts grieved at lamentable, untimely passing of Dorothy Baker, distinguished Hand of the Cause, eloquent exponent of its teachings, indefatigable supporter of its institutions, valiant defender of its precepts. Her long record of outstanding service has enriched the annals of the concluding years of the Heroic and the opening epoch of the Formative Age of the Bahá'í Dispensation. Fervently praying for the progress of her soul in the Abhá Kingdom.

Assure relatives of profound loving sympathy. Her noble spirit is reaping bountiful reward.

Advise hold memorial gathering in the Temple befitting her rank and imperishable services . . .

[January 13, 1954]

Mary Barton

Grieved by passing of your dear mother. Her services highly meritorious. Assure you of fervent prayers for progress of her soul in the Kingdom.

[January 26, 1957]

Victoria Bedikian

Praying for progress of the soul of indefatigable and wholly consecrated promoter of the Faith. Her services are unforgettable. . . .

[July 1955]

Ella Cooper

Deeply grieved at sudden passing of herald of the Covenant, Ella Cooper, dearly loved handmaid of 'Abdu'l-Bahá, greatly trusted by Him. Her devoted services during concluding years of Heroic Age and also Formative Age of Faith unforgettable. Assure relatives, friends, deepest sympathy for loss. Praying for progress of her soul in Abhá Kingdom.

[July 18, 1951]

Julia Culver

Grieve at passing of devoted pioneer of Faith, Julia Culver. Her exemplary spirit, unshakable loyalty, generous contributions are unforgettable. Fervently praying for progress of her soul in Abhá Kingdom.

[January 30, 1950]

Dagmar Dole

Grieved by passing of distinguished, consecrated pioneer Dagmar Dole, whose outstanding record is unforgettable, reward bountiful. Praying for progress of her soul in the Kingdom.

[November 1952]

Homer Dyer

Praying for progress of soul of devoted and zealous servant of the Faith.

[January 26, 1956]

L. W. Eggleston

Grieve at passing of valued promoter of Faith. His historic donation of school highly meritorious, reward bountiful in Kingdom. Deepest sympathy; praying for progress of his soul.

[September 8, 1953]

Harry Ford

Grieve at passing of devoted pioneer Harry Ford, whose death will enrich the spiritual development of foremost center of South Africa. Praying for progress of soul in the Kingdom.

[January 14, 1954]

Nellie French

Deeply regret the passing of valiant pioneer. Long record of her services is highly meritorious. Praying for progress of soul in the Kingdom.

[January 4, 1954]

Louis C. Gregory

Profoundly deplore grievous loss of dearly beloved, noble-minded, golden-hearted Louis Gregory, pride and example to the Negro adherents of the Faith. Keenly feel loss of one so loved, admired and trusted by 'Abdu'l-Bahá. Deserves rank of first Hand of the Cause of his race. Rising Bahá'í generation in African continent will glory in his memory and emulate his example. Advise hold memorial gathering in Temple in token recognition of his unique position, outstanding services.

[August 6, 1951]

Louise M. Gregory

Grieved by news of passing of faithful, consecrated handmaid of 'Abdu'l-Bahá. Confident of rich reward in the Kingdom. Her pioneer services highly meritorious.

[May 29, 1956]

Bertha Herklotz

Grieve at passing of faithful, steadfast servant of the Faith. Praying for progress of her soul in the Kingdom.

[February 16, 1956]

Marie Hopper

Praying for progress of soul of loyal, devoted early believer, Marie Hopper.

[September 11, 1953]

Maria Ioas

Share your grief at passing of esteemed veteran of Faith, Maria Ioas. Soul rejoicing in the Abhá Kingdom at the services rendered by her dear son at the World Center of the Faith in the triple function of Hand of the Cause, Secretary-General of the Council and supervisor of construction of the dome of the Báb's Sepulcher.

[May 1953]

Beatrice Irwin

Grieved by passing of steadfast, devoted, indefatigable promoter of the Faith. Her reward assured in the Kingdom. Praying for progress of her soul.

[March 23, 1956]

Marion Jack

Mourn loss of immortal heroine, Marion Jack, greatly loved and deeply admired by 'Abdu'l-Bahá, a shining example to pioneers of present and future generations of East and West, surpassed in constancy, dedication, self-abnegation and fearlessness by none except the incomparable Martha Root. Her unremitting, highly meritorious activities in the course of almost half a century, both in North America and Southeast Europe, attaining their climax in the darkest, most dangerous phase of the second World War, shed imperishable luster on contemporary Bahá'í history.

This triumphant soul is now gathered to the distinguished band of her co-workers in the Abhá Kingdom; Martha Root, Lua Getsinger, May Maxwell, Hyde Dunn, Susan Moody, Keith Ransom-Kehler, Ella Bailey and Dorothy Baker, whose remains, lying in such widely scattered areas of the globe as Honolulu, Cairo, Buenos Aires, Sydney, Ṭihrán, Iṣfáhán, Tripoli and the depths of the Mediterranean Sea attest the magnificence of the pioneer services rendered by the North American Bahá'í Community in the Apostolic and Formative Ages of the Bahá'í Dispensation.

Advise arrange in association with the Canadian National Assembly and the European Teaching Committee a befitting memorial gathering in the Mashriqu'l-Adhkár. Moved to share with the United States and Canadian National Assemblies the expenses of the erection, as soon as circumstances permit, of a worthy monument at her grave, destined to confer eternal benediction on a country already honored by its close proximity to the sacred city associated with the proclamation of the Faith of Bahá'u'lláh.

Share message with all national assemblies.

[March 29, 1954]

Florence Breed Khan

Profoundly grieve at passing of beloved, distinguished, staunch, great-hearted handmaid of beloved Master. Praying fervently for progress of her soul in Kingdom. Her reward assured. Loving sympathy.

[June 27, 1950]

Edward B. Kinney

Grieve at passing of dearly loved, highly admired, greatly trusted, staunch, indefatigable, self-sacrificing teacher, pillar of Faith, Saffa Kinney. His leonine spirit, exemplary steadfastness, notable record of services enriched annals of closing period of Heroic Age and opening phase of Formative Age of Bahá'í Dispensation. Beautiful reward assured in Abhá Kingdom beneath the shadow of the Master he loved so dearly, served so nobly, defended so heroically until last breath.

[December 16, 1950]

Fanny Knobloch

Grieve at passing of beloved, distinguished, exemplary pioneer of Faith, Fanny Knobloch. Memory of her notable services imperishable, her reward in Abhá Kingdom bountiful, assured, everlasting.

[December 14, 1949]

George Latimer

Greatly deplore passing of distinguished disciple of 'Abdu'l-Bahá, firm pillar of the American Bahá'í Community, George Latimer. His outstanding services during closing years of the Heroic and first epoch of the Formative Ages of the Faith are imperishable. Assure bereaved, dearly loved, much admired mother of my profound sympathy and fervent prayers for the progress of his soul.

[June 23, 1948]

Ruhaniyyih Latimer

Saddened by loss of devoted, staunch promoter of Faith, Ruhaniyyih Latimer; her services are unforgettable. Praying for progress of her soul in Kingdom.

[January 20, 1952]

Fanny Lesch

Deeply sympathize in loss of loyal, distinguished handmaid of Bahá'u'lláh, Fanny Lesch. Present with you in spirit at memorial service. Praying ardently for progress of her soul in Abhá Kingdom.

[April 27, 1948]

Edwin W. Mattoon

Grieved by news of your dear father's death. His pioneer, teaching and administrative services are unforgettable and highly meritorious. Assure you of fervent prayers for the progress of his soul in the Abhá Kingdom.

[December 27, 1956]

William Sutherland Maxwell

With sorrowful heart announce through national assemblies that Hand of Cause of Bahá'u'lláh, highly esteemed, dearly beloved Sutherland Maxwell, has been gathered into the glory of the Abhá Kingdom. His saintly life, extending well nigh four score years, enriched during the course of 'Abdu'l-Bahá's ministry by services in the Dominion of Canada, ennobled during Formative Age of Faith by decade of services in Holy Land, during darkest days of my life, doubly honored through association with the crown of martyrdom won by May Maxwell and incomparable honor bestowed upon his daughter, attained consummation through his appointment as architect of the arcade and super-structure of the Báb's Sepulcher as well as elevation to the front rank of the Hands of Cause of God. Advise all national assemblies to hold befitting memorial gatherings particularly in the Mashriqu'l-Adhkár in Wilmette and in the Ḥaẓíratu'l-Quds in Ṭihrán.

Have instructed Hands of Cause in United States and Canada, Horace Holley and Fred Schopflocher, to attend as my representatives the funeral in Montreal. Moved to name after him the southern door of the Báb's Tomb as tribute to his services to second holiest Shrine of the Bahá'í world.

The mantle of Hand of Cause now falls upon the shoulders of his distinguished daughter, 'Amatu'l-Bahá Rúḥíyyih, who has already rendered and is still rendering manifold no less meritorious self-sacrificing services at World Center of Faith of Bahá'u'lláh.

[March 26, 1952]

Florence Morton

Grieve at passing of faithful promoter of Faith. Praying for the progress of her soul.

[April 8, 1953]

Ella Robarts

Praying fervently for progress of soul in Abhá Kingdom of devoted old believer. Assure you loving sympathy.

[May 2, 1950]

Annie Romer

Grieved by passing of Annie Romer, devoted, able promoter and pioneer of the Faith. Her services have been highly meritorious. Praying for progress of her soul in the Kingdom.

[March 1955]

Fred Schopflocher

Profoundly grieved at passing of dearly loved, outstandingly staunch Hand of Cause Fred Schopflocher. His numerous, magnificent services extending over thirty years in administrative and teaching spheres for United States, Canada, Institutions at Bahá'í World Center greatly enriched annals of Formative Age of Faith. Abundant reward assured in Abhá Kingdom. Advising American National Assembly to hold befitting memorial gathering at Temple he generously helped raise. Advise hold memorial gathering at Maxwell home to commemorate his eminent part in rise of Administrative Order of Faith in Canada. Urge ensure burial in close neighborhood of resting place of distinguished Hand of Cause Sutherland Maxwell.

[July 1953]

Anthony Y. Seto

Grieved by sudden loss of your dear husband, valued, consecrated, high-minded promoter of the Faith. The record of his deeply appreciated services both in America and Asia is unforgettable. His reward is great in Abhá Kingdom. Assure you of loving, fervent prayers for progress of his soul.

[May 7, 1957]

Philip G. Sprague

Heart filled with sorrow at premature passing of staunch, exemplary, greatly admired, dearly loved Sprague. Memory of his notable services as teacher and administrator in North and Latin America imperishable, recompense in Abhá Kingdom bountiful. Praying ardently for progress of his soul.

[September 27, 1951]

Gertrude Struven

Grieve at news. Praying for progress of her soul in the Kingdom.

[December 23, 1954]

Juliet Thompson

Deplore loss of much-loved, greatly admired Juliet Thompson, outstanding, exemplary handmaid of 'Abdu'l-Bahá. Over half-century record of manifold, meritorious services, embracing the concluding years of Heroic and opening decades of Formative Ages of Bahá'í Dispensation, won her enviable position in the glorious company of triumphant disciples of the beloved Master in the Abhá Kingdom. Advise hold memorial gathering in Mashriqu'l-Adhkár to pay befitting tribute to the imperishable memory of one so wholly consecrated to the Faith of Bahá'u'lláh, and fired with such consuming devotion to the Center of His Covenant.

[December 6, 1956]

George Townshend

Inform Hands and national assemblies of the Bahá'í world, of the passing into Abhá Kingdom of Hand of Cause George Townshend, indefatigable, highly talented, fearless defender of the Faith of Bahá'u'lláh.

Agnes Alexander, distinguished pioneer of the Faith, elevated to rank of Hand of Cause. Confident her appointment will spiritually reinforce teaching campaign simultaneously conducted in North, South and heart of Pacific Ocean.

[March 27, 1957]

Roy C. Wilhelm

Heart filled with sorrow for loss of greatly prized, much loved, highly admired herald of Bahá'u'lláh's Covenant, Roy Wilhelm. Distinguished career enriched the annals of concluding years of Heroic and opening years of Formative Age of Faith. Sterling qualities endeared him to his beloved Master, 'Abdu'l-Bahá. His saintliness, indomitable faith, outstanding services local, national, international, his exemplary devotion, qualify him to join ranks of Hands of Cause, insure him everlasting reward in Abhá Kingdom. Advise hold memorial gathering in Temple befitting his unforgettable services and lofty rank.

[December 24, 1951]

Albert Windust

Deeply grieved by passing of much loved, greatly admired, staunch, ardent promoter of the Faith, Albert Windust, herald of the Covenant, whose notable services in Heroic and Formative Ages of the Faith are unforgettable. Assure friends and relatives fervently supplicating for the progress of his soul in the Kingdom.

[March 11, 1956]

Index